Endorsements for
The Stairway to Happiness

《通向幸福的阶梯》名人荐语

If asked, most of us would say we want to be happy. Ask parents what they want for their children and the word 'happy' always comes up.

Being happy is actually quite another matter from wanting to be happy.

This fabulous book breaks down the various stages of happiness, making it much easier to understand the different levels and depths of happiness and how to attain them. It also shows how, paradoxically, the best way to be happy is not to seek it for oneself, which is an act of selfishness, but to bring happiness into the lives of others. Understanding how to do this and making a difference to the lives of our families, friends, children, co-workers and even strangers, is the purpose of this book.

I found it a joy to read and would recommend it to anyone searching for meaning in their life and it's a must for anyone involved with adults' and children's wellbeing.

—Claire Howell, Chief Executive and senior executive coach of REDCO Ltd

如果有人问你最想得到什么，大部分的人会回答想要得到幸福。如果有人问父母最希望自己的孩子将来怎样，为人父母总会提到"幸福"这个词。

保持幸福的心态和想要成为一个幸福的人完全是两个不同的命题。

这本书寓意丰富，作者将幸福拆解成几个阶段，让读者更容易理解幸福的不同层次和深度，学习如何达到这些层次和深度。书中也同时提出，和我们通常的认知不同的一点是，幸福并不是寻找得来的。因为"谋求"本身是一种自私的行为，而自身的幸福是在我们为他人带来幸福的过程中实现的。这本书的主旨就是为了帮助大家了解如何才能做到这一点，为我们的家人、朋友、孩子、同事甚至是给陌生人的生活带来改变。

整个阅读的过程轻松愉悦，我十分愿意向所有寻求人生意义的人推荐这本书。对那些关心成年人和儿童福祉的人而言，这本书是必读的佳作。

——REDCO 有限公司首席执行官兼高级高管导师
克莱尔·豪维尔

What I really like about *The Stairway to Happiness* is how fundamental ideas from philosophy have been made refreshingly accessible and married with modern cognitive psychology practices to provide helpful and valuable guidance on living a happier life while helping others to do the same.

The Stairway's five steps make intuitive sense and the examples from daily life enable the lessons to be put into practice more easily. I very much enjoyed reading this book.

——Mrs Lynn Paine, John G McLean Professor
and Senior Associate Dean for International
Development at Harvard Business School

《通向幸福的阶梯》这本书让我最喜欢的地方在于，作者用令人眼前一亮、一读就懂的方式将哲学的基本思想呈现出来，并与现代认知心理学的实践相结合。为人们过上更幸福的生活，又能同时帮助他人寻找幸福，提供既有帮助又有价值的指导。

书中的五步走很符合直觉，举的例子也都来自日常生活，使得这些方法更容易付诸实践。我非常享受阅读的过程。

——哈佛商学院国际发展高级副院长 John G McLean 教授
林恩·佩因夫人

The Stairway to Happiness is a fascinating, stimulating and inspiring piece of work. I read it all the way through until I finished it at 2 am!

The path of self-discovery within this book is a reminder of what is important, what really matters and what is worthy. It also provides an explanation of what happiness actually comprises and guidance on what to do about achieving it for oneself and for others.

This is a 'must read' for those with curiosity of mind and the courage to ask 'why?'

——Martin Hatcher, Former Executive Chairman, Scansource Communications Ltd and MTV Telecoms

《通向幸福的阶梯》是一部引人入胜、令人振奋、鼓舞人心的作品。我一口气读到凌晨两点看完全书！本书中的自我发现之路提醒人们到底真正重要的是什么，到底什么是值得的。书中也对幸福到底由什么组成做出了解释，引导人们如何为自己和他人实现幸福。 对于那些心中充满好奇并有勇气去问"为什么"的人来说，这是一本"必读之书"。
本书中的自我发现之路提醒人们到底真正重要的是什么，到底什么是值得的。

——Scansource通讯有限公司和MTV电信前董事长 马丁·哈彻

The Stairway to Happiness is a thoughtful and valuable guide for those of us who want to understand what constitutes happiness in life, how this can be accomplished and how to help others.

It is a sophisticated and wise book that combines insights from age-old Greek philosophy with contemporary scientific and psychological knowledge as well as practical advice with day-to-day examples. It also includes spiritual reflections to round off a very enjoyable read.

It is a very accessible book that I look forward to sharing and discussing with many of my personal and professional friends.

—Debbie Jaarsma, Professor Innovation and Research in Medical Education, University Medical Centre, Groningen, Netherlands

《通向幸福的阶梯》给我们这些想要了解什么是幸福、如何获得幸福并帮助他人实现幸福的人,提供了全面周详、独具价值的指导。

这是一本构思精巧、充满智慧的书,结合了古老的希腊哲学、现代科学、心理学知识,并根据日常实例提供了实用的建议。它还涵盖了精神上的思考,带给读者一个非常愉快的阅读体验。

这是一本非常通俗易懂的书。我很期待与我的好朋友还有专业领域的朋友一起分享、讨论。

——荷兰格罗宁根大学医学中心医学教
创新与研究部
Debbie Jaarsma教授

The Stairway to Happiness is a fascinating and novel combination of Philosophy, Psychology and Spirituality. It is where science meets spirituality.

Its strength is that it enables the reader to progress smoothly through these different approaches in a logical way and to learn how they are all connected and aligned with each other in a common message of hope and love.

While the final step, the Happiness of Harmony, is the most spiritual and arguably the most difficult as well as important, the reader is introduced gently and seamlessly into this more esoteric, yet vitally relevant world. She/he is left facing the key questions about who she really is, what her priorities should be and how she should address them. This is a revelation in Human Consciousness.

The Stairway to Happiness provides straightforward and valuable guidance on living a better, more peaceful, more harmonious and happier life. Its insights are refreshing.

As a Life Coach and Spiritual Teacher, I applaud this book and look forward to its extension and development into more and different media formats so as to spread the message as widely as possible and help people awaken to the true reality of existence. There is a real need for people to reconnect with the universe and with their soul and to learn to really live.

—Katey Lockwood, Life Coach and Spiritual Teacher

《通向幸福的阶梯》是本让人爱不释手的书,作者以新颖的手法集哲学、心理学和灵学于一体。这本书就是科学与灵性相遇的地方。

本书的优势在于,读者跟着这种很有逻辑的方式顺利地通过不同的步骤进步,了解这些理论和方法是如何在希望与爱的共同语言中相互关联,相互统一的。

最后一步——和谐带来的幸福是最具灵性,也可以说是最困难、最重要的一步,在作者轻声细语地引导下,读者在不知不觉间进入这个更为深奥却又极其重要的世界。作者把让人深思的核心问题留给了读者：我们到底是谁、哪些事情最重要，应该怎么处理。这是人类意识的启示。

《通向幸福的阶梯》为过上更美好、更安宁、更和谐、更幸福的生活提供了直接而有价值的指导。它的见解令人耳目一新。

作为一名人生导师和精神导师，我很欣赏这本书，并期待它以更多样化的形式在不同的平台上呈现，这样能帮助更多的人从存在的真实里觉醒。现代人确实需要重建自己灵魂和宇宙的联系，并学会真正的地生活。

——人生导师兼精神导师
凯蒂·洛克伍德

Wise, insightful and packed with practical advice, *The Stairway to Happiness* has the potential to transform many lives for the better. It is unusual to find a book on a deep subject such as this which is easy to read and very accessible. I enjoyed reading it a lot and will keep it close at hand.

——Wei Huang, Independent investor and strategist, Shanghai, China

《通向幸福的阶梯》是一本充满智慧和洞察力的书。书中的建议非常实用。这本书很有可能帮助到更多的人过上更美好的生活。很难得能找到这样主题深奥，读起来却又简单易懂的书。我很享受阅读的过程。我会不时拿出来读一读的。

来自中国上海的独立投资人兼策略师 黄伟（音译）

This is a 'must-read' for anyone who has children and loved ones or, like many of us, has lived a life faced with challenges. Vernon shows us grace, acceptance, love and the stairway to a beautiful, fulfilling and happy life.

We will all continue to face challenges in our lives, but with The Stairway to Happiness as our guide, we will come out stronger and better on the other side.

—Joy Atkinson, President, Firmenich Body Home Care North America, USA

对于那些有孩子,有自己爱着的人来说,又或者像我们大多数人一样,每天面临着生活的挑战的人来说,这本书是"必读"的佳作。卫尚凯向我们展示了优雅、接纳、爱的含义,和一道能够通往美好、充实和幸福生活的阶梯。

生活中的挑战源源不断,但在《通向幸福的阶梯》这本书的指引下,我们将在另一方面变得更加强大、更加出色。

——美国芬美意美体护理中心北美总裁
乔伊·阿特金森

The Stairway to Happiness resonates with my own experience in many respects. Combining classical wisdom, theory, theology and psychology with Vernon's own life experience results in an inspiring and yet practical book. I am grateful to have had the opportunity to share it and I have been able to consciously practice the steps almost immediately, not least with the stress of my three children's A level exams!

—The Revd Tina Molyneux, Associate Priest of the Church of England and mother of triplets

《通向幸福的阶梯》在很多方面与我的经历产生了共鸣。这本书结合了经典智慧、理论、神学、心理学和卫尚凯本人的的生活体验,浇筑成了一本鼓舞人心又充满实用意义的书。我很高兴有机会将这本书分享出去。我很快就有意识地开始实践书中提到的方法,帮我应对了三个孩子升学考试的压力!

——英格兰教会 副牧师 三胞胎母亲
蒂娜·莫利纽克斯牧师

The Stairway to Happiness

《通向幸福的阶梯》

Vernon Sankey

[英]卫尚凯

The
Stairway
to
Happiness

通向幸福的阶梯

The five key steps on the Stairway to Happiness
and how to climb them

五个步骤攀登幸福的阶梯

Vernon Sankey

[英] 卫尚凯

Copyright © 2020 by Vernon Sankey

All rights reserved. No part of this publication may be reproduced, stored in or introduced into a retrieval system, or transmitted, in any form, or by any means (mechanical, electronic, recording, photocopying or otherwise) without the prior written permission of both the copyright owner and publisher of this publication. The uploading, scanning, and distribution of this publication via the Internet or any other means without the permission of the publisher is prohibited and punishable by law.

ISBN: 978-1-9995972-6-9 (English with Chinese translation, softcover)
(中英对照简装版)
ISBN: 978-1-9995972-0-7 (English softcover)
(英文简装版)
ISBN: 978-1-9995972-1-4 (English Kindle)
(英文Kindle版)
ISBN: 978-1-9995972-2-1 (English EPUB)
(英文EPUB版)

Improve Your World Publishers Co Limited
出版有限公司
www.improvemyworld.com

Translated by: Li Bei
翻译:李蓓

Book design by Jill Ronsley, Sun Editing & Book Design, suneditwrite.com
书籍设计:吉尔·朗斯利 Sun Editing & Book Design

Front cover concept by Angela Godley
封面概念设计:安吉拉·戈德利

Printed and bound in the United Kingdom
印刷装订 英国

DEDICATION

献词

The Stairway to Happiness is dedicated to those people who have a genuine passion for learning and growing, for helping and creating happiness for others and, in so doing, finding happiness for themselves. They will be people with a compassionate soul, who are kind and respectful, who appreciate what some call 'the little things' but which are what really matter most in life: a smile, a thank you, nature, simplicity, authenticity, friendship, peace, tolerance and love. They understand that we are all part of the same universe, their actions are guided by a sense of justice and truth and they are awake to what is truly 'real' and beautiful. I hope they will enjoy this book.

《通向幸福的阶梯》是献给那些发自内心对学习和成长充满热情，乐于帮助他人、为他人创造幸福，并在此过程中找到自己的幸福的人。这是一群心怀慈悲的人，他们善良，懂得尊重别人，懂得欣赏生活中真正重要的，其他人所谓的"小事"：一个笑容、一句感谢、自然、质朴、真实、友谊、安宁、包容与爱。他们明白我们都是同一个宇宙的一部分，他们的行为受到正义感和真理的指引，他们对真正"真实"和美已经觉醒。 我希望他们会喜欢这本书。

Begin at once to live life
and count each separate day
as a separate life.
　　—Seneca

立刻就开始生活吧，
把每一天
当成
一次不同的人生。
塞内卡

CONTENTS
目录

Acknowledgements
致谢语 ... i

THE STAIRWAY TO HAPPINESS: PART 1
第一部分 ... 1

Why be happy?
为什么要追求幸福感 ... 8

A very brief Greek historical perspective
来自古希腊的启示 ... 11

UNDERSTANDING THE STEPS
幸福的阶梯五步走 ... 27

The First Step: Instant Gratification
第一步：即时满足 ... 29

The Second Step: The Happiness of Achieving
第二步：成就带来的幸福感 ... 37

The Third Step: The Happiness of Giving
第三步：给予带来的幸福感 ... 43

The Fourth Step: The Happiness of Relationships
第四步：人际关系带来的幸福感 ... 53

The Fifth Step: The Happiness of Harmony
第五步：和谐带来的幸福感 ... 69

THE STAIRWAY TO HAPPINESS: PART 2
第二部分 81

The First Step: Instant Gratification and an Introduction to Some Basic Concepts of Cognitive Psychology
第一步：即时满足和认知心理学基础 89

    Habits, attitudes, beliefs and expectations
    习惯、心态、信仰、期待 105

    Where do our attitudes, beliefs and expectations come from?
    我们的心态、信念、期待都从哪里来？ 128

    Using imagination to change the picture
    用想象力助力改变 146

The Second Step: The Happiness of Achieving
第二步：成就带来的幸福感 161

    The importance of self esteem
    自尊的重要性 174

    Setting goals
    目标的设定 179

The Third Step: The Happiness of Giving
第三步：给予带来的幸福感 198

The Fourth Step: The Happiness of Relationships
第四步：人际关系带来的幸福感 211

    Relationships need symmetry
    人际关系需要对称性 213

    Establishing rapport
    建立融洽友好的往来 220

Energy and drive 精力与动力	226
The way information is viewed and assimilated 对信息的接收和理解	234
The way decisions are taken 决策的制定方式	239
Lifestyle management 生活态度的管理	247
Empathy, warmth and sincerity 同理心、热情、真诚	252
Listening and paying attention 仔细倾听	259
Building trust 信任的建立	267
A sense of humour 幽默感	271
Mirroring 镜像模仿	276
Letting go 放手	287
Love 爱	296

The Fifth Step: The Happiness of Harmony
第五步：和谐带来的幸福感　　　　　302

Awareness 认识	309
Acceptance 接受	322

Savouring the moment
活在当下 328

Controlling ego and self-talk
自我控制和自我对话 1 331

Purpose and intention
目的和初衷 337

Wisdom, reverence, compassion and love
智慧、尊重、同情、爱 343

About the Author
关于作者 351

ACKNOWLEDGEMENTS
致谢语

When I set out to write this book, encouraged by my family and friends, I had no idea how much enjoyment I would have and how much I would learn. Nor did I understand what was involved and how much help I would need! None of this could have been done without the kindness and enthusiasm of so many. They have taught me so much.

当我在家人和朋友的鼓励下开始写这本书的时候,我没有想到自己会如此享受写作的乐趣,也没有想到会在这个过程当中学到那么多东西,更没有意识到这其中所涉及多少事情,更没预料过我所需要的帮助。如果没有这么多人的善良和热情,所有的一切都不可能实现。他们教会了我很多。

I am very grateful to my lovely wife and family for their constant support and love, their tolerance and their many valuable contributions. They epitomize so much of what the book is about.

我很感谢我可爱的妻子和家人,感谢他们一直以来给予我的支持和爱,感谢他们的包容和贡献。他们就是本书中核心最好的写照。

I am also very grateful to my friends who, through their awareness, profound understanding and willingness to share have been instrumental in helping me write a book that is based on sound principles as well as set in a wider, more philosophical and spiritual context. They too are wonderful role-models.

我也很感激我的朋友们。通过他们对幸福的认识、深刻的理解、积极地分享,帮助我完成了这本建立在健全的原则基础上,涵盖更广泛理论、包容了哲学、灵性内容的书。他们也是极好的榜样。

All the anecdotes of the happiness of harmony are drawn from personal experiences involving family or friends and are truly heartfelt.

书中所有关于和谐的幸福的故事全部来自于身边的家人和朋友,因此也更为真实感人。

I would also like to thank my editor, Jill Ronsley, for her wonderful work and all her help and advice. It has been a great pleasure to work with someone so positive and professional.

我还要感谢我的编辑—吉尔·朗斯利,感谢她出色的工作和帮助以及建议,能有幸和这么积极、专业的人一起工作是一件非常愉快的事情。

The Stairway *to* Happiness
通向幸福的阶梯

Part 1
第一部分

The purpose of life is happiness,
which is achieved by virtue, living according
to the dictates of reason, ethical and
philosophical training, self-reflection,
careful judgement and inner calm.

Very little is needed to make a happy life;
it is all within yourself, in your way of thinking.
Marcus Aurelius

人生的目的是为了追求幸福,通过遵守美德,经过理性、
伦理、哲学的修炼,不断地自我反思、仔细判断,
保持内心平静来实现。

实现幸福的人生真的不需要太多。
一切都在自己心中,都在于你的思维方式。
马可·奥勒留

A calm and humble life will bring
more happiness than striving for success
and the constant anxiety that comes with it.
Albert Einstein

平静而低调的生活所带来的快乐,
远比成功和追求成功所伴随的持续焦虑更丰富。
阿尔伯特·爱因斯坦

The objective of *The Stairway to Happiness* is to consider the way human beings achieve differing levels and intensity of happiness, why they don't always succeed and what they can do to overcome obstacles and create a powerful and happy future for themselves and those around them.

本书的目的是为了思考人类如何获得不同阶段和不同程度的幸福,探讨为什么幸福如此难觅,寻找幸福的路上如何应对障碍,如何才能为自己和周围的人创造有力而美好的未来。

The Stairway to Happiness is directed at all thinking human beings and is relevant to everyone. It has direct implications for children making their first steps in life as it has for adults of all ages, parents, students, people working in every profession, senior executives, leaders of our communities, the unemployed and the retired.

《通向幸福的阶梯》适用于所有爱思考的个体,适合每一个人。不论是迈出人生第一步的儿童,还是任何年龄阶段的成年人,不论你是为人父母、在校学生、身处任何行业,亦或高管、社群领导、失业也好、退休也好。

It is particularly appropriate for people who are wondering about their own mission in life, what they should do with their life, what future they really want and to what extent their life is a happy and fulfilled one or if they need some help and assistance.

尤其适合那些正在思考着自己人生使命的人。思考自己的人生该做什么，想要有怎样的未来，人生要怎样才幸福美满，抑或在某方面需要帮助或支持。

At a time when we are frenetically rushing about trying to keep up and feeling that we are overwhelmingly lost, we seem to have little time to take stock. And yet it is precisely at such times that we need to do so.

每每感到发疯一样地向前冲，只求赶上别人的步伐，每每感觉压力太大迷失自我的时候，我们最缺的就是抽出时间静下心来重新审视。而事实上，这也正是我们在这种时候最需要的。

The issues raised here are common to everyone and it is simply the manner and intensity with which they manifest themselves that differs. Just as the busy executive in the office needs to acquire the wisdom and skills to manage his life successfully and happily, so does the person at home—not just for themselves but more especially for others.

我们在这里提出的问题是每个人都会遇到的，区别在于发生在不同人身上的方式和强烈程度。置身办公室中业务繁忙的高管,需要获得智慧和技巧更好地管理自己的生活;坐在家中的那个人也一样,还不只是为了他们自己,更是为了身边的人。

In Part 1, we explore the circumstances that create, nurture and promote happiness—the *five key steps*—as well as some of the potential dangers that lie in the way. Many of the situations described will be very familiar.

本书第一部分,我们先探索创造、培养、推动幸福的环境———也就是五个关键步骤,以及一路潜在的危险。相信当中描述的很多情况大家都很熟悉。

In Part 2, we explain how the mind works and some basic principles of cognitive psychology. We also describe and explain a number of techniques and methodologies that can be learnt and successfully deployed to overcome the problems as they occur at each stage of the journey.

本书第二部分,我们进一步阐述思维的运作方式,以及认知心理学的一些基本原理。也会阐述一些可以用来解决每个阶段遇到的问题的技巧和方法。

As in all matters regarding successful outcomes, it is ultimately each person's own desire to learn and achieve change that dictates whether, and to what extent, they will succeed.

纵然每个人都想要获得成功的结果,但具体是否获得预期的结果,到底在多大程度上成功,最终还是取决于个人自身对学习渴望和作出改变的欲望。

While *The Stairway to Happiness* will provide a guide and instructions, it is up to each person to decide to make the necessary effort. It is only through personal desire, effort and determination that change can happen

本书会给大家指出方向和方法,然而真正的努力还要看个人。只有个人的意愿、努力和决心才能真正带来改变。

If it's to be, it's up to me!

改变,掌握在自己的手中!

Why be happy?

为什么要找寻幸福?

Living a happy life does not mean that we have to be happy all the time, wandering about with a benign smile on our faces and living in an unreal utopia. Nor does it mean that we do not feel anger, irritation, sadness or any other human emotion.

幸福并不意味着要每时每刻都要开心,并不是说走到哪里脸上都挂着无公害的微笑,置身于非现实的乌托邦世界。也不是说,我们就感受不到愤怒、烦躁、悲哀,同人类其他正常的情绪绝缘。

Happiness is an emotion that, when allowed to develop and flourish, enables us to make the best of good times, for ourselves and for others. It also helps us to handle adversity, when it inevitably arises, more positively and with better results.

幸福是一种情绪,一旦这种情绪得以生根、发芽,能让我们在幸福的时光里不负当下,为自己,也为他人。也能让我们在不幸无法避免时,以更积极的方式获得更好的结果。

There are many other reasons why happiness is beneficial. Research has shown that happiness generates a wide range of important benefits to health, relationships, achievement, resilience, decision-making, creativity, responsibility and success.

除此之外,幸福的益处还有很多。研究表明,幸福感能为健康、人际关系、成就、韧性、决策、创造力、责任感和成功带来诸多益处。

Happiness also brings benefits to our environment. Research has also shown that happier people are more responsible in their behaviour, take less risky actions, are more attuned to the needs of others and their environment and are more likely to vote and do voluntary work.

幸福感也有益于我们周围的人和物。研究同时也表明,幸福的人群总体健康状况较好,对自己的行为也更加负责,较少采取高风险的行动,更在意周围的人和环境的需求,也更愿意参与投票,参与志愿者工作。

Happiness is also contagious. Happy people lighten the atmosphere and help others around them become happier. A study in the *BMJ* (*British Medical Journal*) found that the happiness engendered by happy people affects others across 'three degrees of separation', and thus has a positive effect on the mood of your friend's friend's friend.

幸福感也是可以传染的。幸福的人能够点亮氛围,点亮周围的人。《英国医学杂志》(BMJ)的一项研究表明:幸福感可以通过"三度分隔"原则从快乐的人向周围传播,也就是说你的幸福感能够影响到你的朋友的朋友的朋友。

Happiness attracts others and, as a result, attracts happier experiences. For that to happen, people need to understand the different levels and intensity of happiness that can exist and how to develop the attitude and skills to, simply, become happier. After all, people are unlikely to attract happiness if they are miserable, unsmiling, uncommunicative, testy or angry!

幸福感也能吸引他人,其结果是叠加出更加幸福的体验。要达到这个效果,首先要懂得幸福的不同阶段和程度,然后运用相应的态度和技巧,变得更加幸福。毕竟,情绪低落、没有笑容、无法交流、焦躁易怒的人是很难吸引到快乐情绪的。

Happiness is about helping people live better lives and creating a society that is healthier, more creative, more generous, tolerant and harmonious. There has never been a greater need for this.

幸福感也源自于帮助他人改善生活,创造更加健康、富有创造力、慷慨、包容、和谐的社会。而当今世界最需要的就是这些。

A very brief Greek historical perspective

来自古希腊的启示

Prior to Socrates, most ancient civilizations tended to have a rather pessimistic view of human existence and their own role on earth. They attributed success or failure to the happiness or anger of the gods, whichever ones they happened to believe in, which, over the centuries, were many.

苏格拉底出现之前,绝大多数古代文明都对人类存在和人类在地球上的角色持悲观态度。把一切成功和失败都归因于天神的喜怒。信哪个神,就是哪个神在主宰成败。几世纪过去,众神更替。

Happiness was therefore a rare event dependent on the favour of the gods. It was not for mere mortals to seek to achieve happiness. This would have been seen as an act of excessive pride—hubris—to be met with retribution and disaster—nemesis.

幸福于是就成了神赐的小概率事件,而非我等凡人可以寻觅获得的。自我寻找幸福会被看作过度自大的狂妄行为,必将招致灾难与报应。

So the gods, rather than the individual, were responsible for whatever happened—a wonderful way to abnegate responsibility for selfish actions. Note that we still use today the expression 'it's in the lap of the gods' when we feel there is nothing we can do.

于是,不论发生什么,都是神的责任,而非个人——无疑成了为自私行为推卸责任的完美方式。以至今天我们还会在感觉自己无力的时候,使用"一切听天由命"(原意为"在众神的膝上")这样的表达方式。

However, the optimistic Socrates was the first known Western person to argue that happiness is attainable, and only attainable, by direct human effort. He advocated turning away from the pleasures of the body and concentrating on the nourishment of the soul by exercising conscious control over desires so as to be able to harmonize the other parts of the soul.

然而,乐观的苏格拉底成就了西方世界(已知的)第一个提出"幸福是可以,且只可以透过人类努力获得"这样论调的哲学家。他倡导人们追寻灵魂的成长而非肉体的享乐。通过有意识地控制欲望,实现灵魂各部分的和谐。

Developed carefully and conscientiously over time while living a moral rather than immoral life, this method would pacify the mind and result in a divine-like state of tranquillity and inner happiness.

认真而有意识的摒弃不道德的行为,遵循道德规范生活,能够平静内心,最终带来内在的宁静与幸福。

Socrates lived during a period of war and deprivation in an environment of cruelty, depravation and ignorance. This led him to question all aspects of his and his fellow citizens' existence and behaviour and raise evident social and ethical issues.

苏格拉底生活在一个战乱、资源匮乏的时代。在这个充斥着残忍、堕落、无知的环境中,他开始向周围的一切提问,开始思考自己和他人的存在、行为,提出一系列社会伦理问题。

Socrates made himself very unpopular in Athens by challenging existing beliefs and preconceptions, most of which he felt were based on myth or rumour and were without logical foundation.

由于挑战当时的传统想法,苏格拉底搞得自己在雅典非常不受待见。而他所质疑的,大多是他认为来自神话和谣传,而非构建在逻辑基础上的理论。

He would admit his ignorance and seek truth through a process of questioning. This was designed to expose ignorance and discover knowledge and wisdom—the basis of happiness.

苏格拉底从不掩饰自己认知的局限,通过提问探寻真相。质疑和探索真相的过程就是暴露无知、发现知识和智慧的过程,也就是幸福感的基础。

His questions were straightforward but uncomfortable. Why do wealthy, high-born Greeks live a life of gluttony, cruelty and selfishness when fellow citizens are dying of disease and hunger? Why is it so important to be moral when we see all around us immoral people who seem to be benefitting more? What, exactly, is happiness? Is happiness to be sought for itself as a virtue or is it the result of achieving 'success'? Or is it something else altogether? What really happens to the soul after death? Does anyone really know?

他所提出的问题直截了当,有时甚至让人不舒服:为什么含着金钥匙出身的富裕阶层过着暴殄天物、残暴自私的生活,而普通民众却死于饥荒与疾病?为什么遵守道德如此重要,而周围都是践踏道德的人,然而他们却活得更滋润?到底,什么才是幸福?幸福是一种美德,需要通过自我探索去找寻吗?还是说幸福是获得成功后的副产品?抑或是完完全全的另外一种东西?人死后灵魂到底会去哪里?有谁真正知道?

All these questions could, of course, be equally asked today.

所有这些问题,当然,都适用于今天。

The price he paid for his open quest for truth was to be sentenced to death for 'corrupting youth'. True to his beliefs, he did not blame the gods for his fate but went cheerfully to his death, which was by his own hand, knowing he had kept faith with his beliefs.

苏格拉底公开寻找真相,为此他付出了生命的代价,以"腐坏青年人"为由被判处死刑。忠实于自己的信仰,他没有责怪天神给自己安排的命运,而是欢喜地赴死。他知道这死也是他自己为了忠于信仰而选择的。

He considered that death represented the ultimate release of the soul from the limitations of the body and continued discussing philosophical concepts with his friends right up to the end.

他把死亡看作对局限于躯体内的灵魂的解放，直到人生终点，都在和朋友讨论哲学问题。

Plato, Socrates' pupil and the person from whom we learn most about Socrates, believed, like his teacher, that human beings must be consciously moral to be truly happy. Immoral people cannot achieve happiness.

苏格拉底的学生柏拉图，是我们了解苏格拉底的重要来源。和他的老师一样，柏拉图相信，人必须有意识地遵循道德才能真正幸福。没有道德的人是无法获得幸福的。

For Plato, being moral meant developing the four cardinal virtues of wisdom, courage, moderation and justice. The wise (not didactic), courageous (not reckless), self-controlled (not manic) and just (not uncompassionate) person is thus at peace, fulfilled and ultimately happy.

对柏拉图来说，道德包括培养智慧、勇敢、节制、正义四美德。要做到明智而非说教，勇敢而非鲁莽，自律而非躁狂，公正而非无情，才能真正达到平静、完满、真正的幸福。

Without justice there can be no peace.

没有正义就没有和平

Given a choice, we all prefer to have a healthy rather than unhealthy body—a perfectly rational point of view. Similarly, our soul needs to be healthy and requires harmony and justice to be healthy.

在有选择的情况下，我们希望拥有健康的身体，这是非常合理的观点。同理，我们也希望拥有健康的灵魂，这就需要通过和谐、正义来获得。

The just soul acquires a psychological harmony that maintains balance whatever the circumstances.

健康的灵魂也需要精神上的和谐，从而抵御周遭变化、维持自身平衡。

Plato distinguished different types or steps of happiness and redefined happiness in terms of internal rather than external characteristics.

柏拉图明确划分了幸福的不同类型和阶段，并用内在而非外在的特点重新定义了幸福。

For Plato's pupil Aristotle, happiness is not an abstract idea but based on personal experience and practical actions, whose ultimate achievement is the discovery of happiness.

到了柏拉图的学生亚里士多德,幸福就不再是一个抽象的概念,而是通过个人体验和实际行动最终获得的成果。

Happiness is the meaning and purpose of life, the whole aim of human existence.

**幸福是人生的意义和目的所在,
人类存在的终极目标。**

Although seemingly self-contradictory, true happiness is not achieved by seeking it for itself. Rather it is the by-product of and depends on an active life filled with positive moral and just decisions.

尽管貌似自相矛盾,但真正的幸福并不是找寻而来的。而是践行道德和正义决策的副产品。

These decisions are taken in the full realization that the individual and the individual alone is responsible for the outcome of each decision and must live with its consequences.

这些决策都是在明确知晓自己行为后果的前提下作出的,决策者个人对每个由他/她自己做出的决定的结果和后果负责。

As these decisions become wiser, more responsible and beneficial, so too the individual discovers new truths, expands his or her consciousness and moves closer to a happier mental state and the happiness of self-actualization.

渐渐的,每个决策都会变得更加明智,更负责任,更有益;决策者会发现更多,觉悟也更高,精神状态上更快乐,更靠近自我实现的幸福感。

Socrates, Plato and Aristotle's thinking also gave rise to another major philosophical movement, Stoicism, which will feature significantly in Part 2.

苏格拉底、柏拉图、亚里士多德的思想带动了另一个哲学思想运动:斯多葛学派。就此我们会在第二章中详细讨论。

Stoicism was founded by Zeno of Citium in Athens in the early 3rd century BC. It was developed by Epictetus, Seneca and the Roman Emperor Marcus Aurelius, the last of the so-called Five Good Emperors, and taken up with enthusiasm during the Roman

Empire and by the early Christians before declining with the development of the Christian Church's own teachings.

斯多葛学派发源于公元前三世纪的雅典,由基提翁的芝诺创立。日后,由埃皮克提图,塞内卡和罗马皇帝马可·奥勒留(即"五贤帝"的最后一任)发扬光大。这些思想在罗马帝国得到繁盛,在基督教教会自己的教条发展起来之前为基督教广泛使用。

Stoicism re-emerges during the Renaissance and again in the modern era. Current cognitive behavioural methodologies and practices have close and direct links to those of Stoicism.

斯多葛学派的理论在文艺复兴时期和现代再次浮现。今天的"认知行为疗法"的方法论和实践都和斯多葛学派的理论有着直接且密切的联系。

Stoicism is a philosophy of personal ethics and a way of life, informed by logic and subject to the laws of nature. This means conducting a virtuous life guided by logic, wisdom, self-control and clear judgment in the face of adversity, in harmony with the divine order of the universe and respecting nature and all people.

斯多葛学派探索的是个人道德和生活方式,主张以逻辑为导向,遵循自然法则。认为人,在遭遇不幸的时候，应当以一种以逻辑、智慧、自我约束、仔细判断的方式有德性地生活，顺从宇宙的秩序，遵循自然之道，尊重人类。

According to Stoic teachings, the path to happiness is to be found in accepting each moment as it occurs, understanding that the only two things we can ever control are our thoughts and our actions and that these should be governed by our self-control, resilience, empathy for fellow human beings and the four cardinal virtues, as espoused by Plato, of Wisdom, Courage, Justice and Temperance.

按照斯多葛学派的思想，幸福之路是从接受已经发生的每一个瞬间开始的。理解我们唯一能控制的两样东西就是自己的思想和自己的行为。这两样东西是由自我控制力，不屈不挠的意志，对人类的同理心和柏拉图定义的经典四美德（智慧、勇敢、正义、节制）来管理的。

According to the Stoics, everyone and everything is a manifestation of the same universe; so human beings should live in peace and harmony with each other, because all men alike are products of nature. Improving a person's ethical and moral behaviour is central to Stoic philosophy, including the control of anger, envy, jealousy and all those sentiments which detract from a happy life.

斯多葛学派认为,每个人、每件事都是同一个宇宙的一种表现形式。因此,人类应当和平共处、和谐生活,因为每一个人,就像其他人一样,都是大自然的产物。斯多葛哲学的核心是改善个人的道德和伦理行为。这就包括对愤怒、嫉妒、羡慕及所有限制个人获得幸福生活的杂念的控制。

***Your life depends on the quality of your thoughts.*
Marcus Aurelius**

人生的质量取决于你思想的质量。
马可·奥勒留

Since the only things we can truly control are our own thought actions, it is by understanding how our mind works and training our thoughts to make judgments in accordance with sound and deeply held values that we can live a happier life.

既然我们唯一能控制的是自己的思想和行为,那么,了解我们思想的运作方式,训练自己的思维方式,让思想学会根据正确的价值观去判断,就能让我们的生活更幸福。

A happy life* lets go *what we cannot control (and which tends to make us stressed and unhappy), focuses on the present and what we* can *actually

achieve, appreciates **what we have** *rather than yearning for what we cannot have and rejoices in the beauty of life.*

幸福的人生需要放手我们无法控制的东西(以及给我们带来压力和不快乐的东西),专注在当下和我们真正能够获得的,珍惜我们所有的,而非期许无法获得的,享受生活的美好。

Seneca mirrors these thoughts when he writes: **'True happiness is to enjoy the present … without anxious dependence upon the future.'** And again: **'It is not the man who has too little, but the man who craves more, that is poor.'**

塞内卡也呼应了这种想法,他写到:"真正的幸福是享受当下…不预支未来的焦虑。""贫穷并不是占有的少,而是欲求更多。"

However, despite this overview of Greek philosophy, *The Stairway to Happiness* is not intended to be a learned treatise on ethics, rather it seeks to explore the levels of intensity and depth of the different types of happiness that human beings can experience against the background of and with the benefit of the wisdom passed down through the ages.

然而,除了对古希腊哲学的回顾外,本书并不想大篇幅地探讨伦理道德,而是探索运用远古流传下来的智慧,人可以体验到的不同程度和不同深度的幸福感。

Throughout the *five key steps*, we see that the thoughts of Socrates, Plato and Aristotle, Epictetus, Seneca and Marcus Aurelius are as relevant today as they have ever been and provide wisdom and direction on what human beings need to master. Human nature has not changed in the intervening years.

在前面提到的五个关键步骤中,我们能看出苏格拉底、柏拉图、亚里士多德、埃皮克提图、塞内卡和马可·奥勒留的思想仍然适用于今天,因为他们提出的是人类需要掌握的智慧和方向。人类本性在这数千年间并未改变。

The teachings of these philosophers remain totally appropriate, although they lived nearly 2,500 years ago. They could be called the first cognitive psychologists in that they sought to understand how the mind works and what processes need to be learnt to achieve understanding, success and ultimately happiness. Socrates said: **'An unexamined life is not worth living.'** The *five key steps* examines an important aspect of life, the search for happiness.

二千五百多年前这些哲学家提出的教义,完全适合今天。他们可以说是第一批认知心理学的专家,不断探索

通向幸福的阶梯 25

思维的运作方式,思索要通过什么过程和步骤实现理解,获得成功,最终得到幸福。苏格拉底说过:"没有经过审视的人生是不值得的。" 这五个关键步骤就是在审视人生重要的一方面,寻找幸福的过程。

As part of that search, *The Stairway to Happiness* offers practical advice, guidance and some techniques that will help individuals determine their own pathway to happiness. In so doing it explores the risks, difficulties and obstacles that will present themselves along the way and provides practical guidance and skills on how to deal with them.

作为这个寻找过程的一部分,本书提出了务实的建议,指导方式和技巧。能够帮助读者选择适合自己的方式。同时,也探讨了一路上可能出现的风险、困难和障碍,并提出可操作的指导方法和办法。

I cannot teach anybody anything;
I can only make them think.

我什么都教不了别人,我只能让他们思考。

It is for the reader to think for themselves and decide their own course of action.

最终,我们需要的是让读者自己开始思考,让读者自己决定他们如何行动。

UNDERSTANDING THE STEPS

幸福的阶梯五步走

THE FIRST STEP: INSTANT GRATIFICATION

第一步：即时满足

When baby is born, she cries. She needs comfort and food. Whenever she cries, she needs something. Once satiated—the very first step of happiness—she (normally!) calms down and goes to sleep. Until, that is, she needs the next thing. As she grows she begins to respond by smiling and, gradually, the needs turn to wants. And crying brings results: the first incidence of instant gratification, the first step of the stairway of happiness.

孩子一出生就会哭。小婴儿需要安慰和食物。只要一哭，就代表需要什么。一旦满足了(也就是迈向幸福的第一步)，婴儿(通常来说)就会安静下来睡觉。直到下一次，有新的需要的时候。慢慢长大，婴儿开始用微笑来回应，逐渐从需要什么变成想要什么。哭泣是会有结果的：这就是最初的即时满足，也是幸福的阶梯上的第一阶段。

As the baby becomes a toddler, child, adolescent, youth, she learns quickly that she can experience some level of happiness by wanting and getting.

从婴儿时期逐渐走向幼儿期,再到儿童时期、青春期、青年期,一个人渐渐会发现,通过不断的想要和获得,能够体验到不同层面的幸福感。

But this happiness is rather short-lived and requires constant topping up. It is also rather shallow in its intensity, without substance or depth.

然而,这种幸福感的存续期很短暂,需要不断地补充。同时,这种幸福感在其程度上也较浅,没有实质或深度上的影响。

The same happens with adults. In a world where it is easier and easier to acquire material objects and borrow money to do so, the happiness of possession or instant gratification is all too easy to achieve. It requires little energy or effort. Just a few clicks.

对于成年人来说也是一样的。现在的世界,越来越容易获得物质上的满足,甚至可以借钱来实现;占有物质的乐趣、即时满足都太容易获得。基本不需要付出多少。只 需要手指一点。

I want. I get. How wonderful!

我想要，我得到了。多么完美！

Only it isn't that wonderful. Yes, it's terrific to have that new toy for a short while. But, like a drug, the effects soon wear off. We get bored with the toy. It goes to the back of the cupboard with all the other discarded items and we forget all about it. Our home is full of such items. They end up in the charity shop, handed down or on the tip.

除非，并没有想象的那么完美。能够得到新玩具，短时间内感觉相当棒。然而，和毒品一样，这种效果消失得很快。我们对到手的玩具失去兴趣，又放回橱柜里，和其他不要的东西归一类，逐渐淡忘。每个人家里都有这类东西。最后从家又到了慈善店，转手给别人。

The happiness we experience is very transient. Is it all that awful? No, not really, even if it is rather wasteful. So what is the real problem?

我们所经历的这种幸福感非常短暂。这有问题吗？没有，即使是浪费也不是问题。那么，真正的问题是什么？

There are two real problems: one is that it is too easy to believe the happiness that ensues, however slight, has value; and the other is where it can lead to, if unchecked.

真正的问题有两个:一个是太容易相信这种满足所带来的幸福感,而且认为这种满足感不论多么渺小,都具有价值;另一个是,这种需求不注意管控,会带来什么结果?

Caught in the spiral of wanting and getting, just like a drug, the opposite of happiness then occurs: we become unhappy if we don't get, feel miserable and look around to see who we can blame for our predicament.

一旦陷进这个"想要"和"得到"交织的循环中,就像染上毒品一样,幸福的对立面出现了:得不到的时候我们就会伤心难过,感到困苦,为自己的窘境找寻可以责备的对象。

Resentment, anger, envy all have space to play their role with significant negative implications for ourselves and our environment.

怨恨、愤怒、嫉妒开始找到发挥的空间,给我们自己和周围带来负面影响。

If our child isn't helped to understand that getting whenever she wants whenever she wants is wrong, we have the makings of the classic spoilt, dysfunctional child. Children need to be helped to learn this as soon as possible.

如果不帮助小孩子建立起"想要什么就得到什么"是"不正确"的概念，那么我们就是在溺爱孩子，塑造功能失调的孩子。这一点是小孩需要尽早学到的。

Instant gratification can have serious downsides. It can lead to addictive cravings, indebtedness, family and marital discord, disharmony.

即时满足可能带来严重的负面影响。可导致成瘾性的欲求不满，家庭和婚姻的不和谐。

Addictive cravings come in many forms but all are the result of the desire for ever-increasing instant gratification that is out of control. Behaviour then becomes compulsive and habitual, the need seemingly insatiable. When added to the pressures of social media, which accentuate the issues, the overwhelming sense of unhappiness can become overwhelming.

强烈的渴望成瘾会以多种方式呈现出来，但其根源都是对不断增长的即时满足失去了控制。当事者的行为变得强制性，习惯性，需求日益无法满足。加上社交媒体的压力，让情况更严重，本来就让人窒息的不幸福感变得更加让人窒息。

In the case of vanity, the need always to appear better, more fashionable, fitter, thinner, and so on brings many risks—from spending excessive sums of money on personal appearance, clothes, diets or surgical interventions to very serious mental problems that require hospitalization.

以虚荣为例,虚荣的表现是总想要看上去更好、更时尚、更健美、更纤瘦,等等等等; 这些需求所带来的风险非常多,比如在个人外表、服饰、饮食上过度花费,甚至需要手术介入,抑或引发严重的心理问题最后需要入院治疗。

It is very concerning to know that unprecedented numbers of young people suffer from depression and other stress-related anxieties.

年轻人受到抑郁症和其他压力相关的焦虑症困扰的数量大得令人惊讶和不安。

What starts off as a perfectly reasonable need to appear smart, healthy, modern and attractive becomes an obsession that takes greater and greater priority, often requiring more and more money to finance, thus causing imbalance, disharmony and unhappiness to the person and those around them.

靓丽、健康、时尚、魅力,本来是完全合理的需求。然而却随着不断的沉迷,其重要性被无限地夸大了,导致人们对金钱的需求越来越大,给其周围的人带来不 平衡、不和谐、不愉快。

This brings us to the question of money. Money is itself neutral. It acquires value only in what it can do or be used for. Acquiring it, or any other possession, just for its own sake is not a path that leads to happiness. How many things do we actually need?

讲到这里,我们得谈谈钱的问题。钱本身是个中性的存在。它只有在使用过程中才能实现自身的价值。有钱,或占有其他财物,本身是并不能带来幸福感的。因此,我们到底需要拥有多少东西?

Although its absence can clearly lead to unhappiness, money in and of itself has no value.

尽管缺钱确实会导致不幸福,但钱本身是没有价值的。

It can, however, be used to achieve worthwhile objectives.

然而,钱,确实可以用来获得有价值的东西。

Socrates said that a wise person will use money in the right way in order to make life better, while an ignorant person will be wasteful and use money poorly, ending up worse than before. Money is only good when used wisely, for a purpose that is beneficial. This is part of leading a moral, balanced existence.

苏格拉底说过,智者把钱花在正处,让生活更美好,而无知者则会把钱用到无意义的途径,其结果比以前更糟。钱只有使用得当的时候才是好的,要用得有意义。这个就是迈向平衡、道德的一步。

Instant gratification, therefore, is a very early stage of happiness with limited value and many downsides. We do derive an element of pleasure from treats, and there is nothing wrong with that. But there needs to be a proper balance to avoid creating the spoilt child syndrome or the stressed-out adult.

即时满足,只是一种相当初级阶段的幸福感,其价值有限, 还附带很多负面效果。奖励确实能给人带来愉悦感,这点本身没有问题。但是,我们需要一种平衡来避免孩子被宠坏,避免奖励变成被压力,压垮成年人。

Human beings need to learn the risks of instant gratification and how to deal with them positively.

我们要充分了解即时满足的风险,积极应对采取措施。

THE SECOND STEP: THE HAPPINESS OF ACHIEVING

第二步:成就带来的幸福感

While the first level of happiness is limited in scope, energy and effect, the second step—the happiness of achieving—has more depth. It requires more effort and its effects are longer lasting. It is also a building block of essential personal development and growth, requiring more energy, application and drive.

虽然幸福感的第一个层面,在范围上、能量上、效果上是有限的,但第二步:成就带来的幸福感更加地强烈。获得这个层面的幸福感需要更多努力,其效果也持续更久。这个层面的幸福感也是个人发展和成长的必要构成要素,需要更多的能量、应用和动力。

Let's go back to our child. She goes to school and begins to learn. She learns to talk, play, sing, dance, and each time she learns something new, she achieves and experiences a sense of happiness, a happiness made greater by the congratulations she receives. She feels good about herself and wants to achieve more frequently.

再回到幼年时期的故事。小孩子去上学,开始学习。学习说话、游戏、唱歌、跳舞……每次学到新东西,就获得并体验到一种幸福感。这种成就感在周围的人的祝贺下得到放大。于是,对自己的感觉更好,想要更频繁地获得成就。

Successful children exude happiness and this has contagious effects on others, who are drawn and attracted to them. This can also incite jealousy from others, often those less able than themselves, so they need to learn new skills to deal with this. These new skills are closely associated with steps three and four.

成功的孩子渗透出幸福感,而这种幸福感是可以感染被它吸引的人。当然也可能招来别人的嫉妒,通常是来自不如他们的人的嫉妒。关于这一点,他们需要进一步学习新技能来应对。这些技能又直接和第三步和第四步相关。

All being well, however, the achievements will continue throughout her life as she succeeds—in concerts, plays, sports and exams and receives awards, diplomas, medals, appointments and promotions.

这些成就感会伴随她一生：音乐会、戏剧、体育运动、考试、得奖、证书、奖牌、任命、升职。

Each achievement will allow her to feel a deeper, longer-lasting level of happiness, which has more value than before. It requires more of our higher efforts to achieve. It requires more intense levels of energy and the ability to set and achieve goals with the attendant skills of imagination and visualization.

每一次取得新的成绩，都能给她带来更深刻的，更长久的幸福感，比上一次更有价值。每一次也都比上一次需要更多一点努力，需要投入更多的精力，同时也需要应用想象力和视觉化的能力设定目标、取得目标。

Who cannot remember a time when they achieved something special, something that required real effort and the pride they felt when they achieved it? It is easy for memories of such events to be recalled many years later with great clarity and a revived sense of pride and satisfaction. This was also the stimulus for more effort and more achievement, leading to more successes.

谁都不会忘记自己取得某个特殊成绩的时刻，那种需要真正付出努力才能得到的结果。这种骄傲感不会被遗忘。这种记忆即使多年后还是容易被唤起，细节清晰，重燃骄傲与满足感。这也是更多努力和成绩的动力，也能导向更多的成功。

At this stage, we should ask the question: what is success? Is success achieving our goals? Is success achieving happiness? Does that mean the greater the success, the greater the level of happiness? Can we in fact be truly happy?

到了这个阶段,我们不禁要问:成功是什么?成功是不是就是达到我们的目标?成功就是获得幸福感?是否意味着成功越大,幸福感越强?是不是可以做到完完全全的幸福?

While the second step—the happiness of achieving—is a major move forward and provides a significantly enhanced experience of happiness, it is not sufficient in itself to provide lifelong happiness or the harmony of the soul that Socrates describes.

虽然在第二步中,通过取得成绩获得幸福感,是重要的一步,能够明显地强化幸福感的体验。但是,其本身却不足够带来终生的幸福感,抑或苏格拉底说到的灵魂的和谐。

The quest for success and its attendant recognition is finite.

对成功的追求和随之而来的认可是有终结的。

Take the successful sportsperson, famous actor or artist, the brilliant politician or the successful business executive, they can only rest on their laurels for so long. The adulation they enjoyed may not last. They are only as good as their last achievement and the disappointment of not being able to continue at such a high level can be devastating. They cannot expect to be happy ever after. On the contrary, as with instant gratification but after a somewhat longer period of time, the happiness of achievement turns to the unhappiness of the 'has-been'.

以成功的运动员、著名的演员或者艺术家、卓著的政客、成功的高管为例,他们已经取得的成就只能维持一段时间。所带来的赞许也不会是无止境的。他们的成绩只止于最后一次的成功,也失望于无法延续这样高度的成就。此后不能再继续这种愉悦。而另一方面,就像即时满足一样,成就所带来的愉快,在一段时间之后,只留下过往的骄傲所带来痛苦。

Unless they learn to step up to the third and fourth levels they will not avoid the emptiness of diminishing past achievements with the dissatisfaction that this brings. There is no such thing as a happy retirement if there is no further activity or purpose: only regret, disappointment, even depression.

除非他们能学会走上第三和第四个台阶,不然无法避免过往成就淡去所带来的空虚感和不满足感。现实中没有快乐的退休这种东西,除非后面有别的活动或目的:不然的话只有后悔、失望甚至抑郁。

Socrates believed that happiness could only be achieved by human effort that is rooted in deep reflection. If we want to find greater happiness, we need to understand deeply where we want to go at whatever stage of life we are. We need to determine what efforts we want and need to make—with our energies, our talents, our lives—to achieve a meaningful future. For this to happen we need to set and reset our goals.

苏格拉底相信,幸福只有通过人类努力来获得,它植根于深深的自省中。如果想要找到幸福,我们必须深入理解自己要去哪里,在生命的哪个阶段。我们需要决定,要付出些什么努力,用多少精力、占多少人生,获得有意义的未来。为此,我们要制定还要不时重新设定目标。

THE THIRD STEP: THE HAPPINESS OF GIVING

第三部：给予带来的幸福感

Acquiring and achieving, the two first steps on the stairway to happiness, are essentially inner directed. They are primordially selfish. They are about wanting and achieving for oneself.

获得和取得，是通向幸福的前两步，也是必须的内在动因。这两个条件初衷是利己的。都是为自己想要和想取得的。

Achieving is about effort and diligence, determination and personal sacrifice—all admirable and necessary virtues and vital for the progress of humankind. It could be argued that these virtues are indeed humanity's very foundation and the essence of progress. All very worthy. There's nothing wrong with that. But there is a major risk.

"取得或者赢取"需要勤勉和努力,决心和自我牺牲,这些都是令人欣赏也是必要的美德,是人类进步的重要美德。也许有人会说,这些美德确实是人类的基石也是进步的必须。都很有价值,完全没错,但这里有个很大风险。

Being essentially focused on the self rather than on others creates an ever-increasing risk of our life becoming out of proportion. This manifests itself in wanting to achieve purely for the personal acclaim and fame it provides or for the sheer accumulation of things, as if a heap of objects is a reflection of an individual's greatness. Achievement risks becoming an exercise in vanity.

只专注于自己,会带来不断激增的风险,导致我们的生活失衡。这种失衡表现在纯粹为了个人的喝彩和名誉而努力,又或者为了单纯数量上的累积。好像收获的东西越多,才能反映个人的伟大。对成就的追求变成了成了对虚荣的追求。

Achieving at all costs, winning no matter what or achieving results in whatever way are traps for the unwise and unwary. This is especially so when 'achieving' becomes 'achieving more than others'.

不惜一切代价获得成就,无论如何都要赢会导致一不留神或不小心就会掉入陷阱。尤其是成绩意味着一定要比别人更好的时候。

At this point, achieving for its own sake becomes manic, stressful and negative, creating unhappiness for the individual and, more particularly, for those around him or her, for whom life can become intolerable.

到这个阶段,取得成就本身成了癫狂、压力、负面、带来不愉快的情绪,给自己也给周围的人,人生变得不能忍受。

There is disharmony of the soul leading to serious health risks, dysfunction and misalignment, burn-out, family and marital problems and unhappiness.

灵魂的不和谐会带来严重的健康问题,导致功能障碍、不适,让身心消耗殆尽,带来家庭和婚姻问题,还有痛苦。

To avoid this and return the soul to a harmonious state, we arrive at the third step, the happiness of giving.

要避免这个结果,得让灵魂回归到和谐的状态。这就来到了第三步:给予的快乐。

This third step is the first one that focuses on others and their happiness, not our own. This is the first step that sees altruism as a virtue. It is next on the stairway and it is the critical step forward.

这第三步其实是把焦点从自身转向别人和别人的快乐的第一步。这是把利他视为美德的第一步。是阶梯上的 一步也是关键的向前一步。

Paradoxically, through the happiness we can bring to others, this is also where we create a higher level of happiness for ourselves.

然而,通过我们给他人带来幸福的过程,也给我们自己创造了更高一级的幸福感。

The happiness of others becomes the focus of our energy. Our own happiness becomes a by-product, but a by-product that has more depth than anything that has gone before.

他人的幸福成了我们能量的来源。我们自己的幸福成了副产品,然而这种副产品的深度超越了之前的。

Having acquired and achieved in the first two steps, the happiness of giving, or giving back, is vital for moving forward. It is also deeper, stronger and much longer lasting.

在前两步获得之后,给予或者回报带来的喜悦,是向前一步的关键,它也比前面两步更坚实持续更久。

Giving becomes more rewarding than receiving—the exact opposite of step one. Not only is the happiness engendered by this more perennial but, once understood and appreciated, it provides a platform for everlasting benefit.

给予比接受更有获得感——这和第一步完全相反。如此带来的喜悦不仅更加持久,一旦被理解和欣赏后,会形成更长久的益处。

Age is not the issue here, but it has everything to do with maturity. Who has not seen children, even small children, help others with small tasks or share their toys? Or even ask an adult, in genuine interest, how they are and how their day has been, while smiling at them and making them feel good?

年龄在这里不是问题,然而却和成熟度有关系。我们都见过小孩子,甚至很小的孩子,在小事上帮助别人,或者把玩具分给别人玩。也可以问问成年人,老老实实说他们最近怎么样,一边问一遍对他们笑着,让他们感觉良好。

Such acts are all acts of giving, where the focus is not on oneself but on another. The so-called small gestures, such as smiling, saying hello, saying please and thank you, giving a seat to an older or infirm person, are as much acts of giving as voluntary work, caring for people or the environment, helping others with their problems, enjoying others' successes, contributing to charities, setting up foundations for worthy causes, and so on.

这一类的举动都是在给予,焦点都不在自己身上而是在他人身上。这就是小的举动,例如微笑,打个招呼,说句请,说句谢谢,把座位让给年老或者不便的人。其他以给予为出发的举动类似志愿者工作,关爱他人,关心环境,帮助别人解决问题,分享别人的成功,捐助慈善机构,建立慈善基金或类似的举动。

If you want to feel happy, do something nice for somebody—it will have its own rewards.

如果想要感觉幸福,为他人做点好事,会给你带来回报。

This is also the first step where human warmth and empathy are manifested directly, qualities that bring support, cheer and, yes, happiness to others.

这也是人类温暖和同理心直接得到印证的第一步,内在带来支持、欢呼还有给予他人的幸福。

All these acts of giving imply giving of oneself. They are the active, conscious, responsible decisions that bring in their wake a level of fulfilment and happiness that is intense and heightened.

这些给予的举动都暗示着个人的付出。个人是主动,有意识,有责任的决定付出,给他们带来一种满足和幸福感,这种幸福感和满足感是强烈和明亮的。

This is what Aristotle means when he says happiness depends on an active life filled with positive, morally responsible actions.

这也就是亚里士多德说的幸福取决于充满积极、有道德的责任感的行动赋予的生活。

There is no room for passivity here. This is about making and taking positive decisions and living with the consequences. It requires great energy and a different way of life.

没有空间留给消极被动。这里的关键是作出主动正面的决定,并且承担后果。这就需要巨大的能量和另一种生活方式。

This is where the most difficult questions start to be asked: 'Who am I?'; 'What do I want to be?'; 'Why?'; 'What are my goals?'; 'How do I want to conduct my life?'; 'What sort of human being do I want to be?'; 'What do I want to leave behind?' These are all questions that test us profoundly and are uncomfortable. They also need to be answered.

于是,最难回答的问题来了:"我是谁?";"我想成为什么样的人?";"为什么?";"我的目标是什么?";"我要怎么样生活?";"我想成为什么样的人?";"我想要放弃什么?" 这些都是深层次检验我们的问题,都会让我们不舒服。但是也需要回答测我们的问题,都会让我们不舒服。但是也需要回答。

For happiness to exist to its full intensity, the answer has to come from deep personal reflection and a conscious list of priorities and goals that, for the third step, require to be both inner and outer directed. How do I want to live my life and what impact can it or will it have on others? How can that impact be beneficial and contribute to the happiness of others?

要想全面感受幸福感,上述这些问题的答案应当来自自己深层的反思和有意识的对其优先重要性的排序。因为第三步,需要内在和外在指引。我要怎样生活,我的生活要带来什么样的影响,怎样影响到别人?这种影响怎样才能是有益的,能够给他人带来幸福的?

Having reflected on our choices, we have to be able to confirm that we have made them 'because this is what I choose to do after proper reflection'. In other words, 'This is my choice,'; 'This is who I am and want to be,'; 'These are my decisions'; 'This is my own commitment and no one else's.'

反思了自己的选择,我们要能够确认我们又选择是"因为这是我们深思熟虑之后的选择"。换句话说,"这是我的选择";"这就是我,这就是我要做的人";"这是我的决定";"这是我自己的承诺而不是别人的"。

Yes, there will be sacrifices, but these sacrifices are willingly and happily accepted since they are the outcome of our serious intent.

牺牲是有的,但是牺牲是自愿的愉快的接受的,因为是我们认真思考后的结果。

Without doing this, we merely drift. Life tomorrow will be much like life today. Nothing much happens and nothing much changes.

没有这些,我们只是在随波逐流。明天的生活会像今天一样。没什么改变,没发生什么。

At some stage in the future, however, we may suddenly wake up and realize that life has passed us by. If everything we encounter in our daily lives is familiar and unchallenging, then our lives carry on automatically and the days seem to fly past, almost at an accelerated pace.

未来的某个阶段,我们可能会突然觉醒,意识到人生就匆匆而过。如果日常生活中面对的都是熟悉和没有挑战的,生活自觉自动的延续,日子就过去了,仿佛是加速逝去的。

Then, at some stage, we'll say: 'Whatever happened to my life?'; 'Where did it all go?'; 'What could I have done differently?'; 'What a waste!'

然后,在某个阶段,我们会说:"我的人生去哪里了?";"发生了什么?";"我怎么才能活的不同?";"虚度了!"

Understanding why this happens, how to manage this process and the techniques to apply to live a purposeful and happier life, lie at the core of Part 2 of *The Stairway to Happiness*.

理解发生了什么,怎么管理这个过程,用什么样的技巧过有意义的快乐的人生。是本书第二部分的核心。

THE FOURTH STEP:
THE HAPPINESS OF RELATIONSHIPS

第四步:人际关系带来的幸福感

The fourth step has many layers and, like an escalator, traverses all five steps. This is the happiness that comes from relationships.

第四步包含多个层面,就像自动扶梯一样,贯穿五个阶梯。这是来自人际关系的幸福感。

By relationships we mean any and all occasions where we interact with others, whether one-on-one or in groups. This includes partners, friends, siblings, family, clubs, associations, teams, companies and all those instances where, by coming together in a relaxed, mutually supportive, open and transparent environment, groups of human beings can create the conditions where each experiences a high level of happiness.

这里说的人际关系,是所有场景下我们和他人的互动,可以是一对一,或者是群体中的。这当中,包括伴侣、朋友、兄弟姐妹、家人、俱乐部、协会社会群体、团队、公司以及所有大家聚到一起,在一个放松的环境中,相互支持,开放,透明的环境,只要有一组人,创造条件,让大家都能体验到一种高水准的愉悦感。

Happiness, in these circumstances, is determined by the quality of the relationships and, most importantly, the trust that exists between individuals. If the level of trust is low, the relationship will inevitably suffer and the opportunity for happiness will evaporate. If, on the other hand, the level of trust is high, the chance of fulfilment becomes that much greater.

幸福感,在这些情形下,是由人际关系的质量决定的,最重要的是个体之间的信任感。如果信任感较低,两边的关系自然不可避免的受伤害,幸福的机会就会消失。如果,幸福感很高,其带来的满足感就会更大。

We need to understand how to build and nurture trust and create an environment where trust flourishes.

我们需要理解如何打造和培育新人,创造一种让信任生长繁荣的环境。

Take our child. Her happiness is dependent on her relationship with, trust in and love of her mother and father or parent or guardian and the alignment and harmony that her parents display.

以小孩子为例。孩子的幸福感依赖于她和父母亲、监护人的关系、信任、爱,以及父母表现出的一致与和谐。

As she grows, her happiness becomes also dependent on her relationship with siblings, friends, classmates, student friends, boy- or girlfriends, partners and work and team colleagues.

随着她渐渐长大,幸福感开始依赖于自己和兄弟姐妹、朋友、同学、学校里的朋友、男女朋友、伴侣以及工作团队的同事之间的关系。

As she learns that this unity and alignment matters, so too she needs to learn how to manage the relationships that lead to harmony. If our child grows up in an environment where trust is absent, she risks growing up frightened, timid, inward looking, pessimistic, unhappy. Her confidence will suffer as will her future happiness.

她会习得团结和一致很重要,于是她需要学会管理自己的人际关系走向和谐。如果小孩子成长在一个信任缺失的环境,她有可能带着恐惧、惧怕、内向、悲观、不悦长大。她的自信心和未来的幸福感也会受损害。

The key then lies in her growing in a trusting, optimistic environment where she can grow healthily and develop autonomy and initiative as she begins to understand the importance of interpersonal relationships.

这里的关键因素是她成长在一个相互信任、乐观的环境。这样的环境让他健康成长、发展出自立能力和想法，开始理解人际关系的重要性。

As she develops her own identity, she learns how to create relationships with people of very different backgrounds, with different viewpoints, energies and dreams in a positive environment.

慢慢地她生成自己的定位，学会如何与不同背景、不同观点和能量与怀揣不同梦想的人建立正向的关系。

She will learn how to say no or disagree in a way that does not cause offence. She will learn how to handle difficult people and situations and make friends easily.

学会如何说不，如何表达不同意，然而又不冒犯他人。学会如何应对难处的人和场景，轻松教朋友。

The Harvard Study of Adult Development, perhaps the longest study of adult life ever undertaken, came up with the clearest message: good relationships keep us healthier and happier. Social connections are vital to life and wellbeing, while loneliness kills.

哈佛对成年人发展的研究，也许是目前对成年人最常期的研究，发现了一下信息：好的人际关系让我们保持健康与快乐。社交互动，对生活和健康至关重要，孤独让人枯竭。

People who have close, warm relationships with their partner, friends, communities and colleagues are happier, healthier and live on average longer than their colleagues who are less well connected and have less well developed relationships.

和父母、朋友、社群、同事之间拥有亲密、温暖的的关系能让这个人更加快乐，健康，寿命也相对其他关系不好的同事要更长。

Although loneliness is often associated with old age, it is not the reserve of older people—far from it. People can be lonely in a crowd or in a marriage. High conflict marriages are toxic for health and often even worse than divorce.

尽管孤独和年老市场关联起来，但这不是老年人的专有名词，绝对不是。人们会感觉孤独，哪怕是在一个群体或者婚姻里。冲突较高的婚姻对健康的危害甚至大于离婚。

It is not the number of friends that a person has, or whether they are, or are not, in a committed relationship that matters, but the quality, warmth and affection of those relationship. The better the relationship, the more protective to health. A similar conclusion was found in a study by the University of Virginia published in the journal *Child Development* on young people from the ages of fifteen to twenty-five.

关键不在于一个人有多少朋友,是否处在一段确定的关系中,而是质量、温暖和这些关系的冷热程度。关系越好,对健康的保护作用越高。相应的结论也在弗吉尼亚大学儿童发展的研究报告中得到呼应。该报告研究了15到25岁年轻人。

Both studies found that not only did good, trusting relationships help protect the body, they also helped protect the mind.

两项研究都发现良好、互信的人际关系不但对身体健康好,对心灵的健康也有好处。

Good relationships are not peaceful all the time. On the contrary, the ability to disagree and argue fervently is fundamental to mutual consideration. Trust, affection and dependability, however, are the keys to good relationships and overcome all arguments.

良好的人际关系不会一路坦途。相反,反对和激烈争论的能力是相互考虑的基础。信任、热爱和依赖性,是建立良好关系,解决所有争端的关键。

There isn't time—so brief is life—for bickerings, apologies, heartburnings, callings to account.
There is only time for loving—
and but an instant, so to speak, for that.
Mark Twain

人生太短,没有时间争吵、道歉、
心碎、吵闹。只有时间爱。
马克.土温

A word about **Love:** Deep relationships are the substance of love and a source of great happiness. The love that partners feel for each other is a source of real happiness, as is the love of parents and grandparents for children and grandchildren or friends for each other.

关于爱,有几句话要说:深层次的关系是爱的基质,幸福感的源泉。伴侣间的爱是真实幸福的源泉,父母和祖父母对子女的爱,朋友间的爱也如此。

In many respects, this happiness is also close to the third stage of happiness, the happiness of giving, in that true love involves giving of oneself and forgiving, trusting and being trusted, caring and being cared for, guiding and helping others and being guided and helped in return.

在很多方面,这种幸福感都愈发趋近于幸福感的第三阶段,给予的喜悦。这是一种全身心给予的真爱与原谅,信任与 被信任,关爱与被关爱,引导语帮助他人,被指引,被帮助。

Love mirrors the five steps. It can be purely about instant gratification. It can be about success. Or it can be about giving and receiving—enhanced by deep caring and accompanied by a sense of peace, harmony and joy.

爱映射出五个步骤。可以单纯表达感恩,也可以是成功,也可以是给予和接受,并由深入的伴随着平和、和谐和喜悦的关怀和陪伴强化。

Love leads to and is also a fundamental part of the fifth stage, the happiness of harmony, beauty and serenity, the love of our world, an understanding that we are all part of a much greater universal truth.

爱能导向第五阶段,同时也是第五阶段的基础,也就是和谐、美、宁静带来的幸福,是世界的爱,宇宙的一部分的爱。

The English language is rich in words to describe complicated emotions and objects with great precision: except for 'love', for which there is only one word.

英语是一门丰富的语言,能够相当准确地形容复杂的情感和对象。然而"爱",却只有一个词。

The Ancient Greeks, on the other hand, had several words for love and would not have understood how we can use the same word to mouth 'I love you' in a romantic setting while casually signing an email 'lots of love'!

古代希腊人,则相反,对"爱"有不同的词可以使用,肯定不能理解仅用"我爱你"三个字在不同的情感场景中表达,也不懂电邮落款写个"爱你"。

In many respects the different Greek words for love relate directly to the different stages of happiness.

希腊语里对"爱"的不同的词汇直接与不同阶段的幸福感相关联。

The first kind of love is *eros*, representing sexual passion and desire. *Eros* provides instant, intense, short-term happiness. But the Greeks considered *eros* potentially hazardous and irrational, leading to disharmony through loss of control, obsession and ultimately pain and suffering. *Eros* is the instant gratification of love, providing immediate happiness that dissipates rapidly and with attendant risks, if it is not accompanied by deeper loving emotions.

第一种爱叫做eros，指的是两性间的热情与欲望。Eros带来的是即时的，强烈、短暂的幸福感。然而希腊人认为，eros具有潜在的危险性和刺激性，失控、占有、痛苦与伤害会带来不和谐。Eros是对爱的即时的感恩，带来即刻的幸福感，如果没有伴随更深层次的爱的情感，则可能消失的很快。

The second type of love is *philia* or deep friendship. This love is the bond found between friends, brothers- and sisters-in-arms, team colleagues and siblings. It is characterized by strong relationships, profound trust and fierce loyalty where friends are prepared to make sacrifices for each other, are willing to share emotions, pain and happiness.

第二种爱叫做philia，抑或深层次的友情。这样的爱是朋友、兄弟和姐妹、同事之间的纽带。它的特点是强大的关系，深层次的信任和忠诚度，朋友愿意为对方牺牲，分享情绪、痛苦和幸福。

The third type, which is along similar lines to *philia*, is *storge*, which is the deep love felt by parents and their children, characterized by similar relationships of trust, devotion, sacrifice and sharing.

第三种,与philia类似的,叫做storge,是父母和子女间的深层的爱。其特点是相似的信任、付出、牺牲和分享。

The fourth variety is *pragma*, the mature love reflecting the deep understanding that develops between partners who have been together for a long time and who have shared many experiences and adventures together.

第四种爱叫做pragma,这是一种成熟的爱,反映出伴侣之间深层的理解。这需要双方相处很长一段时间,共同经历很多,一起冒险之后形成的。

They understand each other completely and know when to compromise, be patient, forgiving and tolerant as a result of the deep love that has grown between them.

作为双方深层次成长起来的爱,双方能够互相完全理解,知道何时让步、如何耐心、原谅、忍让。

Pragma is about giving love rather than just receiving it. It is about making the effort to nurture, maintain and strengthen the loving relationship that deepens and develops over time.

Pragma的给予要大于接受。这种爱更多的是努力了培养、维系、强化双方日渐深化和发展的亲密关系。

Three of these types of love—*philia*, storge and *pragma*—are encompassed in the happiness of relationships, the fourth step on the Stairway.

爱中的三个类型：philia、storge和pragma都包含在人际关系的幸福中，也就是幸福的阶梯的第四步。

The fifth type of love is *philautia*, or self-love. This love has two very different aspects.

第五种爱叫做philautia，亦或自爱。这种爱有两个非常不同的方面。

One aspect, closer to instant gratification, is related to narcissism, where the individual loves themselves, becomes self-obsessed, vain and more focused on personal aggrandizement, fame and recognition.

一方面，接近于即时的感恩，它是和自恋相联系，个人爱着自己，为自己沉迷，自负，更专注于自我的强大、名誉认可。

The other, which is part of the fourth step and closer to self-actualization (see next step), is related to the idea that if the individual is secure in themselves, comfortable about who they are and thus happy about themselves, they will be better able to give love to others.

另一方面,则是接近于第四阶段中的自我实现(见下一步),这是和个体对自我的安全感、舒适感相关的,和他们对自我的认识,是否满意相关。给予的时候这些人会感觉更好。

> ***All friendly feelings for others are an extension of a man's feelings for himself.***
> **Aristotle**

> 任何对他人友善的感情,都是一
> 个人对自己的感情的延伸。
> 亚里士多德

If you do not love (that is, know who you are and have confidence in) yourself, it is difficult to feel love for anyone else.

如果不爱自己(也就是了解自己是谁有自信),很难对别人发展出爱。

Buddhist philosophy refers to this as 'self-compassion'.

佛教中把这个概念叫做"自我..."。

Searching all directions with one's awareness,
one finds no one dearer than oneself.
In the same way, others are dear to themselves.
So one should not hurt others if one loves oneself.
Buddha

在所有方面探索一个人的觉醒意识,就会发现,
自己和自己是最亲密的。同样的,别人也和自己亲密。
因此不要因为别人爱自己而伤害他人。
佛祖

The sixth variety of love is *agape* or selfless, universal love—the closest to the fifth step, the happiness of harmony. This love is extended to all people, irrespective of who they are. It recognizes that we are all part of one universe.

第六种爱是agape或者叫无私,普世的爱—最接近于第五阶段的,也就是和谐的幸福。这种爱可以延伸到所有人,不论对方是谁。这种爱认识到我们都是宇宙的一部分。

CS Lewis called it 'gift love', the highest form of Christian love. In Theravada Buddhism it is 'universal loving kindness'. This is about empathy for mankind and care for all, family and strangers alike. *Agape* was translated into Latin as *caritas* from which we have the word charity.

CS路易斯把这种爱叫做"天赋的爱",基督教最高形式的爱。在大乘佛教(上座部佛教)中就是"普世慈悲"。这是对人类和所有的,家庭和陌生人的同理心。Agape翻译成拉丁语就是caritas,也就是英语里charity(慈善)的原词。

> ***Faith, hope and charity,***
> ***but the greatest of these is charity.***
> **St Paul**

信念,希望和慈善,但当中最伟大的还是慈善。
圣保罗

This fourth step, the happiness of relationships and love, permeates all the other steps and is fundamental to enabling progress to be made from step to step.

第四步,人际关系和爱带来的幸福感,渗透到其他所有阶段,也是从一步进步到另一步的基础。

It provides our existence and world with colour, hope, security and warmth. Even though we may be achieving a high level of happiness through giving, this is considerably enhanced if we supplement it with the happiness of relationships.

这种爱能让我们的存在和我们的世界充满色彩、希望、安全感和温暖。即时通过给予我们能获得高层次的喜悦,人际关系的爱仍然能够强化其他的喜悦感。

The intensity of happiness rises exponentially as we climb the steps and the earlier steps appear very limited by comparison.

幸福的强度随着我们在阶梯上的攀登是呈指数增长的。

THE FIFTH STEP: THE HAPPINESS OF HARMONY

第五步：和谐的幸福

As we have moved up the steps of happiness and reached a very high level at the fourth step, we may feel that this is as far as we want to go, and there is no need to climb any further.

随着我们沿着阶梯不断攀升，到达第四阶段，我们会感受到这就是我们想到的边界，不需要再向高处攀爬。

Indeed, achieving the fourth step provides an intensity of happiness of great depth.

实际上，到达第四级阶梯，就能带来非常强烈和深刻的幸福感。

There is, though, a fifth step—the happiness of harmony—a step that leads still further than the previous four.

尽管,第五级——和谐的幸福所导向的比前面四级更深远。

With the fifth step, and in parallel with the development of our relationships and our experience of the love associated with them, we become increasingly aware that we are part of a much, much greater universe, where there is infinite beauty.

第五阶段,与人际关系和相偕而来的爱共同发展的,我们更加意识到自己是宇宙当中的一部分,到达无尽的美。

In this universe there is beauty everywhere: in people, art, writing, music, sculpture, dance, colours and textures, fragrances, food, plants and animals, the skies at night, rivers and waterfalls, the planets and the infinite twinkling of stars, even in silence.

宇宙中,美是无处不在的。美存在于人、艺术中、写作、音乐、雕塑、舞蹈、色彩、材质、香气、食物、植物、动物、夜空、河流、瀑布、星球和无尽的闪耀的星星,甚至存在于寂静中。

There is beauty all around, if we only take the trouble to see and look, hear and listen, touch and feel.

美就在我们周围,只要我们去看、去听、去触摸、去感知。

This is not intended to be a romantic or new age description of an impossible utopia. The happiness of harmony brings together all the previous steps and adds to it a greater, universal context. It is about taking pleasure in admiring and enjoying what is already everywhere and all around us and which we have forgotten or never had time to really see, hear, touch or experience. It is taking pleasure in the so-called simple things of life.

这种美并不是浪漫或者乌托邦式的爱。和谐的幸福带来的是前面四个阶段的综合,却更强大,放在了整个宇宙的背景下。需要我们再欣赏享受周围的一切,并从中找到乐趣。而这周围的美都是我们可能忘记或者一直没有时间真正去看、去听、去触摸去感受的。也就是从生活的小事中享受乐趣。

In a world where we lead hurried and harried lives and are bombarded by a continuous stream of negative stories, it is understandable we have little time to understand that there are different levels of happiness, let alone have time for happiness at all.

现代生活匆匆忙忙不断充斥着负面的东西。不难理解我们没有多少时间去理解不同层次的幸福,更不用说花时间去感受幸福。

Stop for a minute.

停下一分钟。

The fifth step is a recognition that we are part of something much greater than that which we generally experience and which, if we take time to understand and explore and in combination with the previous steps, leads us to still higher levels of happiness.

第五步是认识到我们是更大的某种东西的一部分,这是我们通常能体验到的,如果我们去理解去探索,加之前几步的配合,能够帮助我们走向更高层次的幸福。

To experience this, we need to develop enhanced skills of being—that is being able, when we choose to, to live in the moment, not worrying about tomorrow or yesterday, to accept ambiguity and that we don't have the answer to everything, (or to anything according to Socrates). It means to experience, quietly and serenely, life all around us—from the simplicity of the flowers in the fields to the magnificence of humanity's greatest triumphs—to learn to use all our senses so as to appreciate to the full all that the world has to offer, to recognize that we are really very, very tiny in the context of our extraordinary universe and to be humble and grateful for what we have.

要体验到这一点,我们需要加强存在的技术——变得有能力,在我们选择,活在当下的时候,不要担心明天或者昨天,去接受这种不确定性,不明确性,接受我们对其他事情没有答案(或者像苏格拉底所说的,对任何事都没有答案)。这就意味着,要体验,静静地,体验我们周围的生活。从最简单的田野中的花朵到人类的伟大——学会使用我们的感官去欣赏世上所有的一切,认识到我们在无尽的宇宙面前是如此的渺小,学会内敛和感激。

Dwell on the beauty of life, watch the stars and see yourself running with them.

沉浸在生活的美中,看看星星,
想象自己奔跑于星星周围。

If we can combine the relationships and love of the fourth step with the beauty, sanctity and harmony of the fifth, we will be close to achieving the self-actualization that is the goal of this step.

如果能把第四步中的人际关系和爱与第五步中的美、明智与和谐相结合,我们就离自我实现更近了,这也就是这一步的目标。

Self-actualization does not have to be about a guru-like transcendental status or involve any mystical sensory powers.

自我实现并不需要像大师那样大彻大悟或者陷入某种神秘力量。

The term 'self-actualization' was coined by Abraham Maslow and in his book Motivation and Personality in which he describes the characteristics of the self-actualized person.

"自我实现"这个说法,是亚伯拉罕·马斯洛第一个开始在他的书《驱动力与个性》中使用,用来形容自我实现的人的特点。

They are people who:

这类人的特点是:

1. are comfortable with and embrace the unknown and the ambiguous;
1. 愿意拥抱未知和不确定性;

2. accept themselves for who they are and know their own flaws;
2. 接受自己本来的面目,了解自己的不足;

3. set priorities and goals and enjoy the journey, not just the destination;
3. 设定优先级和目标,同时懂得享受过程,而非仅仅着眼结果;

4. are unconventional but without seeking to disturb, hurt or shock;
4. 打破传统但不打搅、不伤害、不惊扰;

5. are motivated by personal and communal growth, not by the satisfaction of needs;
5. 动力来自个人和群体的发展,而不只是为了满足需求;

6. have a wider purpose; an unselfish mission concerned with the good of mankind;
6. 拥有更广的目的;拥有包容他人利益的宗旨;

7. work within a framework of values that are broad and are not concerned by trivialities;
7. 有价值观的指导,价值观宏大,不受琐事烦扰;

8. are grateful for what they have and maintain a fresh sense of wonder towards the universe;
8. 懂得感恩自己所拥有的,对宇宙保持新鲜的好奇感;

9. have deep, profound interpersonal relations regardless of class, education, race, colour, political or religious belief;
9. 能够抛弃阶层、教育背景、种族、肤色、政治宗教信仰的不同,与他人建立深入、深刻的人际关系;

10. are humble and keen to learn from people who can teach them something;
10. 谦逊,愿意从他人处学习;

11. are responsible for themselves and make up their own minds based on their own code of ethics;
11. 为自己负责,根据自己的道德标准做决策;

12. are not perfect!
12. 不完美!

Perfect human beings simply do not exist and it would be a very colourless world if they did.

完美的人本身就不存在,如果有,那么这个世界就会黯然失色。

Many of the characteristics of self-actualized people are those evoked in the previous steps, such as setting goals and priorities, developing strong relationships and being responsible adults.

自我实现的人的很多特质都在前面几章中提到了,例如懂得设定目标和优先级,与人建立坚实的关系,做负责任的成年人

In the fifth step, self-actualization is about enjoying the journey and learning to enjoy and find real happiness in the simple but wondrous occasions provided by the universe.

通向幸福的阶梯   77

在第五步中,自我实现指的是享受整个旅程,学习如何享受,在宇宙赋予的简单的奇迹中找到真正意义的幸福。

There is great happiness to be experienced in the world: in a walk with a partner, friend or family along the beach in the evening, listening to the waves breaking on the shore, smelling and tasting the fresh, ozone-rich air while admiring the clouds on the horizon; at a picnic with family or friends on a hillside in the country, enjoying the view of the river and hills beyond, listening to the happy sounds of the children and feeling the warmth of the grass as the heady, fragrance of the lavender wafts all around; at a lively dinner with friends in a relaxed atmosphere in which there is parity of esteem and a shared feeling of fun and warmth; lying on the ground in the late evening looking at the twinkling stars and constellations in the infinite expanse of space; or just a walk in the park or reading a good book under the trees; the warm embrace and cuddle with a loved one; a family reunion where all the members share in a magical sense of warmth, togetherness and love; and in almost anything that has beauty, calm, serenity and love.

这个世界上有很伟大的需要去体验的幸福感:和伴侣、朋友、家人走在夜晚的海滩,听着海浪拍打海岸,细细品味新鲜充满臭氧的空气,欣赏地平线上的云朵;和家人、朋友坐在乡村的山坡上野餐,享受河边的景色和山丘的美景,听着孩子们的欢声笑语,感受青草的温暖,薰衣草令人陶醉的香气环绕;和朋友享受活跃的晚餐,轻松的氛围里大家享受着同等的尊重,一起感受愉快与温暖;躺在公园地上夜深的时候看着闪烁的星星,遥望无尽空间里的星座;走在公园里,树下读一本好书;和爱的人温暖地拥抱依偎在一起;家人的团聚,全家分享者魔幻的温暖的感觉,团聚与爱;任何有美、平静和爱的东西。

Là, tout n'est qu'ordre et beauté,
Luxe, calme et volupté.
'L'invitation au voyage' from *Les Fleurs du Mal*
—Charles Baudelaire

那里,一切都有序而美丽,奢华、安宁、令人愉快。
夏尔·波德莱尔《恶之花·遨游》

By using their imagination and visualization, everyone has the capacity to learn how to find and experience peace, tranquillity and happiness in simple, free, yet often overlooked situations and circumstances. Everyone can learn, like Socrates and the Stoics, to transpose themselves into what is, in effect, another world, an inner world they can inhabit whenever they want to and whenever they feel the need to escape the so-called real external world in order to find harmony, peace, happiness and their own paradise—either by themselves or with other like-minded souls. It's not a place so much as a state of mind or wonder.

运用想象力和视觉化，每个人都有能力学会如何在简单、自由、时常被忽略的情况和环境中找到并体验和平、宁静与幸福。每个人都能学会，像苏格拉底和斯多葛学派那样，把自己传送到另一个世界，内心的世界。一个自己任何时候都可以走进去，逃离外部真实世界的港湾。在这里可以找到和谐、平和与幸福，找到属于自己的天堂，不论是与自己还是和相互欣赏的人一起。这并不完全是某个地方，而是一种心境。

I have deliberately not raised any such specific theological or theosophical matters even though they are, of course, entirely pertinent to this subject. The reason is that, whatever our religious beliefs, we are all seeking to find and experience happiness. *The Stairway to Happiness* is intended to be complementary to and not in conflict with any peace-loving religion nor is it intended to offend anyone. It does not suggest that any particular theology is more or less appropriate. That is up to individuals to decide.

我刻意地没有提到这类专门的神学或神智学的问题，尽管确实和这个主题相关。其原因是，不论我们的宗教信仰是什么，我们都在寻找幸福感的体验。本书的目的是辅助这个过程，而非与热爱和平的宗教相抵触，也不是为了冒犯谁。因此并没有提到任何特定的神学,是比较合适的。这点留给读者自己去决定。

However hard it is to believe at times, all religions seek to find true happiness in one form or another. Most religions have their version of 'heaven', the ultimate place of peace—from *Brahman*, *moksha* and nirvana to paradise, the 'celestial kingdom' and the New Jerusalem.

不论有多难相信,所有的宗教都是为了寻找真正的幸福。大多数宗教有他们自己的"天堂",也就是最终获得和平、宁静的地方—不论是叫Brahman, moksha, 涅槃或者天堂。天界的王国,或者耶路撒冷。

Earth has no sorrow that heaven cannot heal.
Thomas Moore

没有天堂抚平不了的悲伤。
托马斯.莫尔

The Stairway *to* Happiness
通向幸福的阶梯

Part 2
第二部分

Socrates said: 'The unexamined life is not worth living.'

苏格拉底说过:"没有经过审慎的人生是不值得的。"

In Part 1, we examined:

在本书第一部分,我们审视过:

1. what happiness is;
1. 幸福是什么;

2. why it is so important;
2. 为何幸福如此重要;

3. how Socrates and his successors viewed happiness;
3. 苏格拉底和他的学派对幸福的认识;

4. what the five different and ascending steps are;
4. 五个上升阶梯是什么,有什么不同;

5. what each step can provide in terms of intensity, duration and quality as we climb the stairway.
5. 随着我们在通向幸福的阶梯上不断攀爬,每一阶段在强度、持续期间、质量上会带来什么不同。

We also explored the benefits and some of the many pitfalls that can occur on the way up the steps and learnt the importance of effort and achievement, giving back, relationships and enjoying all the things that we have rather than those we do not have but mistakenly yearn for and then stress over.

我们也探索了拾级而上的益处和陷阱,学习了努力和取得成绩,回馈他人,人际关系,和享受周围一切的重要性。

> *We need to learn to desire what we*
> *already have; then we will have all we need.*
> *Love that only which happens to thee*
> *and is spun with the thread of thy destiny.*
> *For what is more suitable?*
> **Marcus Aurelius**

> 我们要学会欲求我们已经拥有的,
> 这样就能获得我们需要的。
> 爱你所有的,和命运给予你的。
> 还能有什么更合适?
> 马可·奥勒留

In Part 2, we will see what understanding, skills, techniques and methods we need to acquire and develop in order to gain the most from each step and unblock obstacles as we move up.

在第二部分中,我们会看到需要用来获得和发展的理解、技巧和方法,从而获得每一步的最大效用,移除障碍,继续向前。

We need to learn these lessons for our own health, wellbeing and inner harmony so as to be better able to manage, appreciate and enjoy our lives through all its vicissitudes—the ups as well as the inevitable downs.

学习这些课程是为了自己的健康、状态和内在的和谐,这样才能更好地管理、欣赏、享受生活,在变迁和不可避免的苦难中前行。

Perhaps more especially, we need to learn these lessons for the sake of those around us whose happiness is also our responsibility. This is also our opportunity to do good things, to teach others what we learn, to make, appreciate and enhance our environment and to make others happier.

也许,更特别的事,我们可以学习这些课程,为了我们周围的人,让他们更快乐也是我们的责任。这也是我们做件好事的机会,教会别人我们学到的东西。从而欣赏、强化我们周围的环境,让周围的人更幸福。

The subject of happiness is by no means a new subject and libraries are filled with self-help books, magazines and pamphlets with a vast range of recipes, suggestions, systems and recommendations. Many are indeed excellent, based on sound principles and contribute to understanding. I have found, however, that it is not always easy to relate the advice provided to specific issues and the bewildering array of suggestions are at times either too complicated or too simplistic to enable the reader to make real progress or understand **why** they might or might not be progressing, **what** the issues really are that they should be tackling and **how** to go about addressing them.

幸福这个话题,已经不是新闻了。图书馆放满了自我学习的书籍、杂志、小册子,还有大量的秘方、建议、系统和推荐。很多都很优秀,都有实实在在的理论原则,容易理解。然而,我发现,要把这些建议放到自己身上,和具体的问题上,却不容易。要么是这些建议太复杂了,要么太简单,没法让读者真正取得进步,理解为什么他们有或者没有在进步。这当中真正的问题是,他们要怎么面对和解决这些问题。

Part 2 of *The Stairway to Happiness* seeks to provide practical advice to enable the reader to:

本书的第二部分寻觅寻找务实的建议帮助读者:

1. understand **why** certain patterns of behaviour occur and re-occur, in other words to understand

what is happening in the mind and how the mind functions;

1. 理解为什么某些特定模式的行为会发生或再次发生，换句话说，要理解思想里的变化和思维功能；

2. learn what to **do** to address these patterns of behaviour and change them if required.
2. 学会如何解决这些行为模式，必要的时候作出改变。

The guidance provided in Part 2 is based on personal learning and experience and on methods that have been tried and tested over many years in a variety of circumstances and with a variety of customers—from comprehensive corporate change programs to one-on-one coaching.

第二部分中提出的知道建议是基于个人学习和体验的。很多方法都饰演过多年，在不同的场景和不同的客户中，从企业到一对一辅导都有实验过。

Hopefully you will find that a dose of common sense has also been liberally sprinkled!

希望你能够找到启发和方法。

Some of the guidance is directly related to specific issues in individual steps and some is 'transversal', in the sense that the processes and skills are relevant across all the steps.

某些知道办法直接针对某个特定问题,有些事可转换的,和其他步骤相关的。

THE FIRST STEP:
INSTANT GRATIFICATION AND AN INTRODUCTION TO SOME BASIC CONCEPTS OF COGNITIVE PSYCHOLOGY

第一步：即时满足和认知心理学基础

Before we look into each step, we need some basic background understanding of what happens in the mind, why and how.

了解每一步之前，我们需要了解一下内心的一些基本知识，知道一下原理和机制。

Let us take our baby again. She cries whenever she needs food, comfort or changing and mother or father obliges. As she develops, she learns very quickly, subconsciously, that crying produces results.

再回到婴儿时期看看。婴儿需要食物、需要安慰或者换尿布,需要母亲或者父亲的时候就会哭闹。日渐发展,她很快下意识的学会,哭闹能带来结果。

This is the first manifestation of instant gratification. Although this is subconscious it is still very relevant and is necessary, natural, instinctive and beneficial to baby's survival, growth and development.

这是即时满足的第一个表现。尽管潜意识里,这个需求和婴儿的生存、成长与发展息息相关,非常必要,也是自然而然,天生的有益处的。

But baby also needs to learn, fairly quickly, that Mum or Dad are not 'on tap' every minute of the day and night (at least after the initial few days!). This is good neither for her nor her parents and if this pattern of behaviour and expectation persists, problems will soon ensue. Why?

然而,婴儿需要学习,而且要尽快的学到,父母不是白天黑夜随叫随到的(除了刚出生的最初几天)。如果这种行为模式和期待值一直持续,对孩子和父母都没有好处,问题立刻会显现。为什么呢?

Here comes the first opportunity to learn something important that goes across all the steps.

通向幸福的阶梯

这里是学会一个贯穿所有步骤的重要事情的第一个机会。

Our subconscious mind controls almost everything that we do.

我们的潜意识控制着机会所有的东西。

Our subconscious mind is the automatic internal controller of our lives. It is permanently on duty and, based on the knowledge it has acquired and is constantly acquiring from us, directs our actions and activities without our having to even think about them.

我们的潜意识是自动的内部控制系统。这个控制器恒动永远在运转。基于它获得的知识和从我们这里不断持续获得的知识，指挥着我们的行为和活动，这个过程都不需要我们思考。

That is why we do not have to think to get out of bed, switch the alarm off, get washed, brush teeth, get dressed, drink our coffee, go to work, say hello, smile, attend meetings, go home, put out the rubbish, switch on the TV or look at our messages. We do it all automatically.

这种机制让我们不需要思考就能起床，关掉闹钟，洗漱，刷牙，穿好衣服喝咖啡，上班，问好，微笑，参加会议，回家，丢垃圾，开电视，查看简讯。这些全是自动自觉做的。

You only have to look at the faces of fellow commuters to realize that most are on autopilot and will probably have little or no recognition of the journey after it is completed.

你只需要看着周围通勤人员的面孔就能意识到，大多数人都在自动驾驶，可能都基本没有或者完全没有认识到旅程已经完成。

Sometimes we try to override our subconscious mind but fail to do so. How many times, for example, have we consciously decided *not* to do or say something—'I won't raise that subject,' 'I won't send that text,' 'I shouldn't talk about x,'—only, a few minutes later, to say or do that very thing?

有时我们试图驾驭自己的潜意识，但是会失败。有多少次，比如我们下意识的决定不要做什么不要说什么。"我不会提这个事情，""我不会发这条短信，""我不应提到，"—短短几分钟之后，就做了说了这件事。

That is because our subconscious mind, which is a fast and powerful learner and designed to help us and keep us 'normal', is leading us in the way it believes we want to go based on our previous actions and pattern of behaviour—otherwise known as our habits, attitudes, beliefs and expectations.

这是因为,我们的潜意识,是一个快速有力的学习者,它的存在是为了帮助我们保持"正常",引领我们根据我们过往的行动和行为模式,向着它相信我们要去的方向。也就是我们的习惯,态度,信仰和期待。

Moreover, our subconscious mind cannot process a negative, so trying *not* to do something will not be helped by our subconscious mind—quite the opposite—with the result that the thought remains in our mind and we act on it a little later, when our conscious mind has moved on to something else.

此外,我们的潜意识不能处理否定的东西。因此尝试不做某事并不能得到潜意识的帮助—恰恰相反—结果是这个想法留在我们脑中,稍后当我们的意识转移到另一件事的时候,再行动。

(Everyone knows if you ask someone *not* to think of a pink elephant, this is precisely the thought that will be come into in their mind as the negative cannot be processed by the subconscious.)

(每个人都知道,如果叫你不要想粉红大象,就会去想,因为我们的潜意识不会处理否定的东西)

Only occasionally do we truly consciously override our subconscious mind and decide on a different course of action. This is usually accompanied by some discomfort, increased energy and stress.

只有偶尔我们的意识凌驾于潜意识的时候,我们会决定作出不同的行动。这时常伴随着不适感,带来能量和压力的增加

The subconscious mind learns very quickly from what we do and develops patterns of behaviour that we call habits—repetitive and reinforcing thoughts and actions that become second nature.

潜意识会很快从我们做的事情和发展出的行为模式中学习,这也就是习惯—重复、加强思维和行为成为了第二天性。

The subconscious also learns our attitude towards things, how we approach issues and subjects, what our beliefs are, based on the information we have hitherto absorbed and filtered, and what expectations we generally have, again based on our experience and the information we have gleaned from all sources.

潜意识也学会了我们对待事物的态度,如何解决问题,学到了我们的信仰,根据我们吸收和过滤的信息和平时的期待,根据我们的经历和我们从不同渠道获得的信息学习。

As these habits become ingrained, they become more difficult and take longer to shift or change. They become automatic.

渐渐地，这些习惯变得根深蒂固，变成了我们的一部分，调整或者改变越来越难也需要更长的时间。

As we become unconsciously competent it is easy for us to rely on these habits and to act automatically without much additional thought or mindfulness.

随着我们无意识地完善，我们日趋依赖这些习惯，开始自动，而不需要多少想法和思考的行动。

There is, of course, great value in this. It is vital for most of the everyday actions we have already described and it keeps us sane and operating efficiently.

当然，这是具备很重要的价值的。因为这对我们每天的行为至关重要，这点我们已经描述过，而且能让我们保持冷静高效运作。

If we did not have such automatic habits, we would be having to learn everything as if it was new each time, which would be mind-destroying as well as exhausting.

如果没有这些自动养成的习惯，每次有新东西就得把所有东西重新学一遍，这样对心智是破坏性的也很劳累。

But our habits have their disadvantages and risks too and our habits, attitudes, beliefs and expectations can also be less than beneficial.

然而我们的习惯有它自己的劣势和风险。我们的习惯、态度、信仰、期待都可以没有好处。

They may, over the course of time, have become either too risky or too risk averse, too bold or too timid, too aggressive or not aggressive enough, based on real-time information or out-of-date assumptions.

有可能,随着时间推移,要么会带来风险,或者太规避风险,太大胆,太小心,太激进,太不够激进,根据实时的信息或者过时的假设。

When circumstances change or evolve, as they inevitably do, or when faced with entirely new events or challenges and we need to make different decisions or judgments or change course altogether, we may simply and lazily rely on the information conveniently stored in our subconscious mind. We may not take the trouble to stop and think properly and drift into an inappropriate or even disastrous decision, based on previous but now no longer relevant experience.

随着环境变化情况转变,不可避免的都会遇到新的事件或挑战。我们需要用不同的决策或评判能力或者完全改变，可能简单的或者懒惰的依赖下意识中储存的信息。可能不愿意耗费精力停下来好好思考，根据先前获得但已经不适应时代的经历，做一个不合适甚至灾难性的决定。

If we sometimes wonder why we keep making the same mistakes or getting the same results, the cause may be right there. We are not taking the trouble to properly assess our situation and are relying too much on our subconscious mind to direct us based on previous information. Unfortunately, the subconscious does not always have the right data to do this well. And so we keep making the same errors. A description of insanity is 'doing the same thing and expecting a different result', and yet that is what we keep doing.

如果我们偶尔想一下为什么自己会犯同样的错误或者得到同样的结果，其原因有可能就在这里。我们没有花时间好好的处理现在的状况，过多的依赖于潜意识根据以前的信息给我们的指导。不幸的是，潜意识并不会永远能获得正确的数据。于是我们犯着同样的错误。对不正常的一种描述就是："做同样的事情，期待着不同的结果"，然后我们一直重复着这个过程。

The information we hold in our subconscious may be entirely inappropriate or wrong (GIGO = garbage in, garbage out) thus ensuring an automatically generated erroneous response.

我们潜意识里获得的信息也许完全不合适或者根本就是错的(GIGO=garbage in, garbage out),如此一来,确保自动生成了错误的反应。

We should also ask: how did the information that we hold in our subconscious get there in the first place? Who put it there? Was it the result of careful study or experience or wise counsel? Or was it what we read in a paper or magazine, inherited from the views of our parents, heard from friends or saw on social media or a Twitter feed?

我们也应该问:潜意识中的信息一开始是从哪里来的?谁放在那里的?是认真研究的结果还是体验的结果,亦或咨询的结果?或者是我们读报纸读杂志来的,从父母的观点哪里继承下来的,朋友那里听到的,或者社交媒体,Twitter上看到的?

And how do we know the information is valid anyway?

我们如何知道这些信息是有效的呢?

We don't! And yet we rely on it to make our decisions.

不知道!而我们还靠着这些信息帮我们做决定。

There is the case of the young, talented man from a less privileged background, who had the ability and the grades to go to university. He refused the place. When asked why, he said because his parents had said, 'People like us don't go to university. What will our friends say?' The well-known book, film and musical, *Billy Elliot*, exposes similar preconceptions.

这就像年轻有才的来自稍稍不显优势的背景,有能力有成绩可以上大学。他却拒绝了入学。别人问他为什么,他说,因为父母告诉他"像我们这样的人不上大学。想想朋友会怎么说?"著名小说《舞动人生》(原名《Billy Elliot》,后改编为同名电影和音乐剧)表达的就是类似的概念。

Our subconscious reverts to its pool of acquired experience every time we plan to do something.

我们的潜意识在每次我们计划做某事的时候,就回退到它需获取经验的储存库。

Unless we consciously decide otherwise, and this takes significant effort and energy, our subconscious mind will effectively decide for us. And all this happens without our being aware of it.

除非我们有意识的决定,而有意识的决定需要耗费很多努力和精力,我们的潜意识会更有效的为我们做决定。这一切都发生在不知不觉中。

Most of the things we do each day, we do subconsciously and automatically and we become very **predictable** because the pattern is ingrained and automatic and others can perceive our behaviour patterns easily because they have first-hand experience of them and may well have been their victim. The expression 'reading someone like a book' is a reflection of this predictability.

我们每天做的事情中的大部分,都是潜意识和自动完成的。因此我们变得很容易被预测,因为行为模式是固定自动的,别人可以从我们的行为模式中轻易的观察出来。因为他们有第一手的经验,可能已经受到过影响。这句表达"像读一本书一样了解某人"就是对这种预测性最好的反应。

If we have developed the habit of being on time for appointments or engagements, this becomes very predictable (and vice versa, of course!). So if we are on time for an engagement and we think we're running late, we feel uncomfortable and stressed, our energy and body temperature rises and we automatically speed up.

如果我们培养出的习惯是守时,这个习惯就会很容易被预测(反之亦然!)。如果我们习惯了准时赴约,我们觉得自己有点晚了的时候,就会觉得不舒服,觉得有压力,我们的精力和体温上升,自动加速。

Our subconscious mind is aware that, given current behaviour, we're going to be late and is activating our bodily responses. The **dissonance** that our subconscious mind feels is translated into a physical response of increased heat and energy.

我们的潜意识是知道这一点的,让当前的行为,也就是快要迟到这个事情,刺激身体的反应。这种潜意识中不和谐感转化成了物理反应,导致温度升高能量爆发。

Our subconscious mind has acquired this behaviour over time and assumes this is how we want to be. It pushes us in the direction it thinks we want to go.

我们的潜意识要求这种行为,也假定这就是我们想要做的。于是,推动我们往这个方向行事

In the case of the person who has acquired the habit of always being late, there is no such dissonance and thus no heat, energy or stress created since none are needed as the subconscious assumes being late is okay, because it always has been for this particular person.

一旦这个人养成了迟到这个习惯,就不会有这种不和谐,也就不会有体温升高,精力增加和压力增大的感受,因为我们需要潜意识假设迟到是可以的,因为迟到对这个特定的人来说一直是常态。

Changing such a habit or any habit is difficult precisely because it entails retraining ourselves; that is, **retraining our subconscious** to a new way of thinking, behaving and acting, changing practices that have been second nature for years.

改变这样的习惯或任何习惯都不容易,因为这意味着要重新训练自己:也就是,重新训练我们的潜意识,以一种新的方式思考、行事、表现,改变经年形成了第二天赋的实践。

Changing habits cannot be done quickly either.

改变习惯是不可能很快实现的。

It requires time, thought, imagination, vision, energy, goals, repetition and determination.

需要时间、思索、想象、视野、能量、目标、重复和决心。

New Year's resolutions rarely last further than the 2nd of January precisely because these steps have not been properly considered, let alone correctly set up. The chances of success are negligible.

"新年志向"(New Year's resolution) 很少延续到一月二日的原因,就是因为没有思考过具体的落实的步骤。更不用说建立起来。成功的几率可以忽略。

Let's come back to baby. Her subconscious mind becomes attuned very quickly to what happens under different situations. She (her subconscious) learns quickly that positive things happen when she cries. Her subconscious has stored this information and it comes helpfully to the surface anytime something is needed.

再回到小孩子的例子。她的潜意识很快地按照不同情形下发生的事情进行调整。她，亦或她的潜意识很快学会，一哭就会有好事。于是，潜意识就把这个信息储存下来，只要有需求，这个信息就跳出来帮忙。

If we as parents do not take the opportunity early on to influence baby's subconscious, by, for example, establishing systematic routines for sleep, feeding and play, which her subconscious then stores for future reference (a positive habit), then baby's subconscious will simply assume that it's fine to cry anytime, anyway, anyplace because it always gets results.

如果我们，作为家长不在早期抓住机会影响孩子的潜意识，比如说，建立系统性睡眠、饮食、游戏的节律，这些习惯小孩子会在潜意识中储存起来用做以后借鉴（正向行为），那么这个孩子的潜意识会自动假定任何时候、任何地点、任何方式哭起来都会有结果。

And a habit will quickly become ingrained that is not desirable, as many unwary parents have discovered!

习惯很快会变得根深蒂固,就像很多大意的家长所不愿见到的。

It can be very frustrating and stressful for parents and is not healthy for anyone. It becomes even more negative for baby too, whose subconscious picks up the emotions of its parents without being able to process them.

其结果会让父母沮丧压力倍增,对任何人都不健康。对孩子也是负面的,孩子的潜意识感受到父母的情绪却没能消化情绪。

What began as instant gratification and a source of happiness for baby, has become a problem for baby and parents.

一开始的即时满足本来是幸福的来源,然而却变成了孩子和父母的问题。

So establishing, early, a coherent, stable and regular pattern of behaviour that is beneficial and healthy, as well as caring and warm, filled with cuddles, play and loving attention is a dynamic way of creating an environment of harmony and happiness.

因此,早期建立其一个连贯的、稳定的、规律的行为模式,是有益而且健康的。它和关爱与温暖,抚摸、玩耍、爱的关注一起,构成了创造和谐与幸福的道路。

This is then positively stored in our baby's subconscious, as well, let's not forget, as that of parents (and grandparents!).

这个过程在孩子的潜意识中正面的储存起来,也不要忘记,对父母(祖父母)而言也是如此。

Habits, attitudes, beliefs and expectations

习惯、态度、信仰、期待

All this holds equally true for our children as they grow up. They need to be encouraged to develop good habits early—a task that requires kindness, patience and firmness—so that they can store these in their subconscious mind whereupon they become automatic.

所有这些因素,在儿童成长过程中都一样重要。孩子需要被鼓励,在养成好的习惯——这是一个需要善良、耐心和坚忍才能完成的任务——这样他们才能把这些储存到自己潜意识中,形成自动机制。

Whenever a situation then occurs where they need to make a decision, armed with their good habits, their subconscious will help them make the right choice.

一旦到了需要做决定的时候,好的习惯、潜意识会帮助他们做正确的决定。

This applies to almost anything they do: being polite, being kind, being positive, smiling, having good manners, doing their homework, crossing the street when the green man lights up, playing nicely with siblings and friends, giving and receiving hugs.

这也适用于大多数情形任何事情：有礼貌、和善、积极正面、微笑、有教养、做作业、绿灯亮的时候过街、和兄弟姐妹友好相处，接受并给予拥抱。

If they can develop the habit of doing these things, so that their actions are natural and an intrinsic part of who they are, then they will have a much greater chance of being happy and creating happiness for those around them.

如果能形成这些习惯，他们的行为就是自然而然的，也成了他们自己的一部分，就更有机会幸福、也为周围的人创造幸福感。

Life, of course, is not always blissful. Nor should it be! Life, like fate, happens and negative, sad, difficult, dangerous, unfortunate events can and will occur.

人生，当然不会一路美好。也本不应该是！人生，就像命运，世事难料，有负面、有伤感、有困难、有危险、有不幸。

It is not so much what happens to us that matters but how we deal with it

发生什么远没有我们怎么应对来的重要。

Armed, however, with good habits, the right attitude, a clear philosophy of life and inner strength, as well as appropriate skills, we are much better equipped to handle both good and bad things.

用良好的习惯、正确的态度，清晰的人生哲理和内在力量武装自己，加上合适的技巧，我们就能更好地处理一切，不论遇到好事还是坏事。

***Life is either an exciting adventure or nothing.*
Helen Keller**

人生要么是令人惊奇的冒险，要么什么都不是。
海伦·凯勒

Helen Keller became blind, deaf and dumb when she was nineteen months old as a result of an acute illness, yet lived a magnificent and full life helping and inspiring others, learning to ride, chairing societies and enjoying life to the full.

海伦·凯勒在自己19个月大的时候因为急病导致失明、失聪、智障,然而却通过帮助他人、激励他人度过了精彩和完满的一生。学会了骑马,管理社团,享受生活。

She was the first deaf-blind person to earn a Bachelor of Arts degree and became an author, political activist and lecturer.

她是第一个获得学士学位、成为作家、政治活动家、演说家的聋哑人。

How often have we met or heard of people with serious problems, illnesses or disabilities who are nevertheless positive, energetic, cheerful, helpful, caring and, yes, exude happiness?

我们是不是经常能见到或者听到这样的故事:那些患有严重障碍、严重疾病或者残疾的人依然保持着乐观精神、精力充沛、助人为乐、关爱他人,甚至还能释放着幸福感?

At the other extreme, how often have we met people who would appear on the surface to have every advantage, blessing and opportunity, yet who, nevertheless are consistently miserable, envious, depressed, depressing and unhappy?

另一个极端是,很多人表面上占据优越性,机会很好,然而,却一直痛苦、嫉妒、压抑、抑郁,不快乐?

In the case of Helen Keller, she was determined, from a very early age, to find a way to communicate and break through her almost total isolation. In this she was brilliantly helped by the wonderful Anne Sullivan who coached, encouraged and inspired her with immense patience. The habits of determination, drive and resilience were instilled from the start with remarkable success.

以海伦·凯勒为例,她很有决心,在很小的年纪就找到了沟通的方法,打破了所有的孤立。当然这方面她接受到了安萨利文的帮助。安以巨大的耐心教导她、鼓励她、激励她。决心、动和坚韧这些习惯都是成功的起点。

In the sorry case of the person with everything but who continually moans and complains, no such early habits were instilled.

一直抱怨的人,早期就没有建立起这样的习惯。

On the contrary, such behaviour is most likely the result of parental neglect, compensated by guilty acquiescence, giving way to any and all demands for the sake of peace and thus helping to instil a habit that will persist into adulthood, unless seriously addressed.

与之相反,这样的行为,最常见的是因为父母亲的忽略造成的,代偿性的出现愧疚的默许,对任何要求,乃至所有的要求让步,只为求得平静。这样的做法,除非严肃对待,否则会建立一种一直持续到成年时期的习惯。

Not only will this attitude have damaged the prospect of a happy life, it will also have damaged the likelihood of a successful one. Who wants to hire someone who moans and complains, blames others when things go wrong and is consistently miserable?

这样的态度不仅会破坏实现幸福生活的可能性,也会破坏获得成功的可能性。谁会愿意雇一个一出现问题总是在哀嚎、抱怨、指责他人,每日惨兮兮的人。

Instilling or acquiring new good habits always requires time, patience, resilience, desire and effort. It requires constant **repetition** so as to create a new way of life that becomes an automatic response.

沉淀,获得新的好习惯通常需要时间、耐性、韧性、欲望和努力。需要持续的重复,才能创造出新的生活,建立自动反应机制。

> *When force of circumstance upsets your equanimity, lose no time in recovering your self-control and do not remain out of tune longer than you can help. Habitual recurrence to the harmony will increase your mastery of it.*
> **Marcus Aurelius**

通向幸福的阶梯

如果周围环境的外力打破了你内心的平静,
一定要立刻恢复自我控制,
一定要适时调试。
习惯性地回归和谐能增加你对和谐的掌控力。
马可·奥勒留

Personal, quality time needs to be spent with our child in a caring and positive environment. This is often very difficult for working or single parents. If affordable, a good childcare professional, or nursery, working in tandem with the parents can be of significant help.

我们应当与小孩子亲自相处,在关爱、积极的环境中享受高质量的相伴。这对于工作的父母或者单亲家庭来说非常困难。如果有可能,专业的儿童看护、幼儿园,辅助父母的办法会有巨大帮助。

And even with the greatest efforts of kind and caring parents, it can be very trying and frustrating. What parent has not had to cope with the 'terrible twos', when our child is learning, subconsciously, to develop her own autonomy and, in the process, refusing to cooperate on practically anything?

即使是付出了最大的努力去慈爱、关爱的父母,也可能精力挫折。父母们都经历过可怕的两面性时期,也就是小孩子正在学习,潜意识中形成自主能力,同时拒绝配合任何事情。

Extreme patience is required as well as a clear understanding between the parents working together as to what is and is not acceptable or negotiable.

父母间需要极度的耐心和清晰的理解才能一起分辨哪些可以接受,哪些是不能接受不能妥协的。

This stage soon passes, to be replaced by new and different challenges.

这个阶段很快就会过去,替代它的是新的不同的挑战。

Our child learns to take initiatives (three to six years) and seeks the approval of peers. She becomes industrious (six to eleven years) wanting to achieve school goals successfully. Then comes a tough period when she develops her identity (twelve to eighteen years) as puberty affects how she sees herself and the world and seeks to discover who she really is.

小孩子会学会主动(3-6岁间),然后需求同伴的认可。她在6-7岁间更加有想法,想要在学校成功取得目标。而后在发展自己认识(12-18岁)间经历一段痛苦。青春期影响了她看待自己和世界的关系,寻求发现真实的自己。

During this time, as parents we are aware that we seem to spend significant time saying 'no' to our child as she experiments and seeks to discover new things.

在这个时期,父母亲清楚我们很多时候都在和孩子说"不",因为他们在尝试试验发现新的东西。

Here comes another opportunity to learn something useful:

Research has shown that parents say nineteen times 'no' for every time they say 'yes'.

借这个机会,我们又能学到新的一点:

> 研究人员发现,父母每说1次"好",
> 都会伴随19次"不"。

In addition, when a child does something wrong parents sometimes *criticize the child* directly, not least if the negative behaviour happens frequently—which it will!

此外,孩子做错事情的时候,父母又是会直接批评,至少是针对负面行为时常发生的时候。

Parents often also assume that if a child does not show promise in any particular activity, it means the child must somehow be 'bad' at it and *always will be*.

父母经常假定如果孩子没有在任何行为上表现出承诺的话,就意味着会一贯的不好。

Nothing could be further from the truth of course, and, in most cases, such judgments are made much too soon and at much too young an age to have any validity whatsoever.

实际与此相去甚远。大多数情况下,这类的评判都下得太早,孩子太年轻都无法得到验证。

But these judgments, often spoken out loud or implied by someone whose opinion they treasure, affect the child and her subconscious, damage her self-esteem and limit her expectations of herself.

然而这些评判,经常都是大声说出来,或者是孩子很看重的对象嘴里说出来的,对儿童的潜意识影响很大,伤害了自尊心,限制了孩子自己对自己的期待。

The effect is often much greater than the parent either felt or intended. An unintended slight, casually delivered by a parent and not intended seriously, can nevertheless deeply hurt our child.

这种效果通常要比父母自己感觉或意想的影响要大得多。无意间的轻轻的,随意地从父亲或母亲那里发出的,本意并不严肃的话,可以深深地伤害到孩子。

It has been found, with adults undergoing behavioural coaching, that such an off-hand slight, uttered carelessly to them many years before by an unwary parent, was the cause of anxiety and trauma at a later date.

事实也发现,成年人接受行为上的辅导,发现很多时候他们的焦虑和伤害是来自早年父母不经意的一句话,却带来了后期的效果。

We need to be exceptionally careful about the words we use.

我们需要特别的关注自己的用词。

Small wonder, then, that children frequently grow up with negative thoughts about themselves and the world. This colours their attitude, beliefs and expectations about themselves and the world they live in.

小的奇迹,小孩子伴随着对自己和世界的负面思想长大。渲染了他们的态度,信仰和对自己及自己生活的世界的期待。

It also impedes their learning and development and discourages them from taking initiatives, trying new things, exploring possibilities, in case they should fail and hence disappoint.

同样也会妨碍到学习和发展,因为担心失败和失望,降低他们的主动性,消磨尝试新东西的可能,扑灭他们去探索可能性的愿望。

In our coaching, we have frequently come across situations where expectations are raised too high too soon, with the result that the child is set up to fail through no fault of her own. She then risks becoming dependent on others, feeling guilty that she is not good enough and inferior compared with her schoolmates.

我们辅导的时候,经常会遇到这样的情况。很多期待定得太高,定得太早。结果是,错不在孩子,但孩子因此而失败。自此之后孩子就变得依赖别人,感觉愧疚,觉得自己不够好,低其他同学一等。

At the other end of the spectrum, parents sometimes attribute skills and competences to their child that they simply don't yet have. This instils in our child's subconscious the idea that they are much better than they actually are with the result that their minds are closed to learning, because they believe they already know.

而另一类父母,则是给孩子套上了他们并不具备的技能和能力。让孩子的潜意识里认为,他们要比自己实际更好,相信自己已经什么都懂了,从此关闭心门,不愿学习。

And when reality eventually happens, they are in for a shock and experience exactly the same, if not an even higher, sense of failure.

等到现实让他们惊醒的时候,其结果都是一样,如果不是更糟,至少是失败的感觉。

In order to help our child move from a world of instant gratification to one of achievement, here are various key learnings:

为了帮助孩子从一个即时满足的世界移到需要取得成绩的世界,有很多关键点:

1. **Say and especially show you love your child frequently. Avoid criticizing her directly. It is her behaviour you do not love, not her.**
1. 经常向孩子表达你爱她。避免直接批评。你不爱的是她的行为,而非她。

Parents love their children and always will. If the child thinks that her parents do not love her—and say so in frustration—they will, at the very least, damage her self-esteem.

父母爱孩子,也会一直爱。如果孩子认为她的父母不爱她,特别是在挫折的时候这么说,他们会至少,损伤自己的自尊心。

It is not the child that should be criticized, but the behaviour. Say instead: 'I love you, and always will, but *I do not like this behaviour. It is not worthy of you because I know you are capable of doing better.*'

应当被批评的,并不是儿童,而是行为本身。比如,可以换一种说法:"我爱你,不论如何都爱你。但是我不喜欢你这种行为。我觉得你可以做的更好。"

2. Role model the behaviour you want.
2. 用你的行为给孩子做榜样。

It seems obvious, but children need role models and the most obvious and best one should be the parent. Nobody is perfect or needs to be, but if we want our child to behave in a certain way, we need to show them the way and do this consistently. If we do the opposite, we should hardly be surprised at the result.

不言自明的道理,但是小孩子需要榜样,最直观最好的榜样就是父母。没有人是完美的,或者说没有人需要变得完美,但是如果我们希望小孩在某方面如此如此这般表现,我们就要让他们看到如此这般行为,而且持续看到这样的。如果我们的行为是反向的,那么其结果毫无疑问不会是自己希望的。

3. Make children responsible for their actions and decisions. Children given responsibility usually act responsibly.
3. 让孩子们为他们自己的行为或者决定负责。孩子给予的责任后通常行为上更负责。

Children are very good at taking on responsibilities when encouraged to do so. They like being responsible for something and thrive on it. They are also much happier and more motivated, as we all are, when the decision is theirs and they are in control.

儿童如果受到鼓励的话,在负责任方面会做的很好。他们喜欢为某事承担责任,努力完成。而且也会更开心更受鼓舞,其实我们大家也都如此。自己能做决策的时候自己可以控制。

When the opportunity arises, or when they seek permission to do something, ask them *what they think they should do* and wait for a reply.

有机会的时候,或者寻找许可做某事的时候,问一下他们觉得自己应该做什么,等他们自己回答。

If whatever it is they wish to do is positive or helpful, all well and good. If it isn't, start over by asking what they would like to do that would be positive as *you want to treat them as grownups*, which means they will be in charge.

只要他们想做的事情是积极的,有帮助的,是好事,那就让他们放手去做吧。如若不然,就先问问他们想做什么。这样做的好处是,你在把他们当作成人来对待,他们可以自己做主。

This turns the situation around and instead of the parent having to come up with ideas and solutions, the child has to do the thinking work and, in so doing, also learns to think for herself.

这样做能反转局势。让孩子开始思考,而不是依赖父母想办法、想方案。这样做孩子就能学会自我思考。

At times, this will lead to some frustrations, especially for the older child, adolescent (or adult!) who may say 'tell me what I should do' when they should be able to work out for themselves.

有时候,有些情形让人沮丧,特别是对年纪大一些的孩子来说,比如处在青春期的或者成年的孩子。本该由他们自己想办法做决定,却还要问父母"我该做什么"。

It is almost as though they do not wish to take responsibility for their own actions, preferring to have the option to blame someone else if things don't work out later.

仿佛好像是他们希望不要为自己的行为负责,这样的话一旦什么地方出错,可以有机会把责任转嫁给他人。

Resist the temptation to tell them what to do.

一定要抵住诱惑不要告诉他们该怎么做。

The correct reply is 'I know what I would probably do if it was me, but it's not me, it's you. It's your life and it's your responsibility to make that decision. No one can or should make it for you. What I can do is show you what to consider in making that decision, *if you want.*'

正确的回复是:"我知道如果是我的话会怎么做,但现在面对问题的不是我,而是你。这是你的人生,也是你的责任去做抉择。没有人能够,也没有人应该为你做决定。

Again the responsibility is shifted back and forces them to think while reducing dependency and encouraging self-confidence.

责任又再次转到了他们身上,迫使他们一边思考,一边减少依赖程度,同时又鼓励了自信。

That does not mean that parents should not make suggestions. Of course they should. But there is a way of doing this that can provide helpful information rather than being somewhat manipulative, which our children will detect immediately.

并不是说父母就放手不管了。当然要给予建议。然而只是在提供有用的信息的前提下,而非指手画脚。不然的话孩子也能立刻察觉出。

Children like to be like their older siblings and friends and, if so, we should help them, gently and carefully, to achieve just that, while being vigilant about allowing one child more favours than another or imposing a younger child on older siblings.

小孩子喜欢模仿大一点的孩子或者朋友,如果有这种倾向的话,我们应该帮助他们,用温柔、细微的方法,要做到的话,必须要保持警觉,给予一个孩子照顾较多的时候,或者让大孩子陪着更小的孩子玩。

By asking questions calmly and carefully, a sensible action plan can be arrived at that has the buy-in of child and parent. It is amazing the extent to which this can make life easier all round.

通过冷静仔细的提问,我们就能在父母和孩子身上落实这个合理的行动。其效果很惊人。

What should one do about laptops and electronic games?

电脑和电子游戏怎么办呢?

Computer games can be fun and come under the category of instant gratification. Like all instant gratification, it provides a definitive happiness fix and buzz, but one that is likely to be shallow and short-lived. It requires frequent topping-up and becomes time consuming and time wasting. The risks are the same for children as for adults. In limited doses, it can be relaxing and fun. In more extensive doses, it is highly damaging.

电子游戏很有趣,也可以归为即时满足一类。就像很多即时满足的例子,它能给到一次的快感,一剂缓和效果。但是却很短暂也肤浅。需要持续的添加,于是就变成耗时、废时的结果。其风险对儿童和成人都存在。剂量有限的时候,可以起到放松和趣味性的作用。过量的话, 破坏性很大。

Not only does it waste time that could be better employed doing other things, it is also essentially unsocial, even antisocial. Looking at an electronic screen for a long time is also unhealthy in its effects on the eyes and brain and can impede sleep.

不仅浪费了本可以用来做其他事情的时间,同时也割断了社交联系,甚至是反社交的。长时间盯着电子屏幕不仅对眼睛和大脑不健康,还妨碍睡眠。

Because it can be so addictive, children (and adults) generally find it hard to limit themselves and this becomes another less helpful habit.

因为可以沉迷，儿童和成人都会发现限制自己的游玩时间很难，玩游戏变成一个越来越没有好处的习惯。

It is also clear that such habits are carried into adolescence with worrying effects. Who has not seen, in a café or fast food outlet, a table of adolescents all looking at or playing with their smart phones and hardly ever looking up, let alone indulging in conversation?

这样的习惯会被带到青春期，带来令人担忧的效果。大家都见过，在咖啡馆或者快餐店，一桌子的年轻人都低头玩手机，基本不抬头，更不用说相互交谈。

We need to instil new habits **early on** by establishing rules, time plans for when to use or not use electronic media and encouragement to develop alternative more constructive activities, such as games, a love of books, cooking, and so on.

我们需要逐渐在早期灌输新的习惯，建立心规则，时间 规划，何时使用、何时不使用电子媒体，鼓励和发展其 他替代性更有建设性的活动，比如玩游戏，看书，烹饪的兴趣，等等。

Above all, we need to get children to the point quickly where they understand **why** they need to limit their time and do so out of their **own free will**.

最重要的是,让小孩子很快理解为什么要限制他们的时间,从而自觉自愿的减少时间。

Their own strength of character should be gently encouraged and applauded and the benefit of having their own mind needs to be developed.

他们自主的能力应当被不时地鼓励和赞许,让他们自己做决定的好处可以慢慢显现出来。

These positive habits will also act as a valuable safeguard to them when peer pressures mount as they grow up, which they will with a vengeance.

这些正向的习惯会保护他们,哪怕是在同伴压力的情况下。

By having strong values, they will be much better equipped to handle the enormous pressures and stresses that they will face as adolescents and have the strength of character not be swayed or drift mindlessly with the herd.

这种强大的价值观建立起来后,他们就会能够在价值观的武装下对抗青春期可能遇到的巨大的压力。有能力不被群体的意志改变或者动摇。

And if their relationship with their parents is such that they are comfortable and happy to talk through their worries and fears in an open **non-judgmental environment before they become real problems**, so much the better. Parents need to make themselves **accessible and good listeners**—major skills in themselves.

如果他们和父母的关系是彼此舒适,可以在非评判的环境中在问题发生之前畅谈担忧和惧怕的,那就更好。父母需要让自己能让人靠近,成为好的听众,这是非常重要的技巧。

> *It is the nature of the wise to resist pleasures, but the foolish to be a slave to them.*
> **Epictetus**

智者的天性会抵抗快乐,然而愚者会成为快乐的奴隶。
埃皮克提图

In an age of conspicuous and mass consumption, it is all too easy to lose sight of what we truly need, as opposed to what we are told, on a daily basis, that we should have for our happiness—the latest gadget or fashion item, the latest thing that will transform us instantly into the person we really should be.

在这个不加掩饰的大众消费时代,很容易迷失忘记自己真正需要什么,而只是听从别人告诉自己,自己需要什么。每天如此。好像拥有了最新款的时尚配饰就会幸 福。最新款能够即可把我们变成自己真正的模样。

The built-in obsolescence, the beautiful images, the invitation to a dream, the peer pressure, the constant bombardment of advice on how to be up-to-date and not left behind are massive temptations for instant gratification and designed to be so. But do we really need any of them?

必定会退化的机制、魅力的想象,进入梦境的邀请、来自同伴的压力,外界繁多的关于如何跟上时代,不要掉队的建议,都是即时满足的诱惑,本身也是为此目的而设计。问题是:我们真的需要这些东西吗?

If there were **no other people to impress**, would we really make the same material choices we make? Would we live in the same house, have the same car, wear the same clothes and buy the same gadgets? Would we be so quick in allowing materialism to overcome spiritualism quite so easily and completely?

如果我们不需要取悦任何人,我们还是会做出这些物质上的选择吗?还是会住在同一座房子,用同样的车,穿同样的衣服,买同样的设备?还是会那么快的让物质主义那么轻易地,完整地占据精神世界吗?

Wealth consists not in having great possessions, but in having few wants.

财富并不在于占有很多,而是欲求有满。

Where do our attitudes, beliefs and expectations come from?

我们的心态、信念、期待都从哪里来?

As with our habits, they all come from our own lived experience of the world, from our approach to life in general and from the say-so of others.

我们的习惯,都来自我们自己对这个世界的体验和经历,来自我们我们对生活的方式,和别人的反馈。

Do any of our attitudes, beliefs and expectations represent the truth? The answer is they represent the truth **only as we believe it to be, or as we have been led to believe it to be, not as it really is**.

我们的心态、信仰和期待是否符合真理?答案是:如果我们相信,他们就符合真理,亦或我们被引导了相信如此,而非真的如此。

By attitude we mean the way we approach an issue. Do we generally have an attitude of openness to ideas and suggestions or do we approach issues more sceptically? This can be changed fairly rapidly.

信仰指的是我们视之为真理的东西,我们对某事的存在的接受程度和信心,亦或是绝对的,特别是在没有证据的情况下。这点需要较长时间才会改变。

By beliefs we mean the things we hold to be true, our acceptance and confidence that something exists or is absolute, especially when there is no proof. This takes longer to change.

信仰指的是我们视之为真理的东西,我们对某事的存在的接受程度和信心,亦或是绝对的,特别是在没有证明的情况下。这点需要较长时间才会改变。

By expectations we mean the assumptions we make about likely outcomes. This will be conditioned by the degree to which we view the world optimistically or pessimistically. This can be changed fairly quickly.

期待指的是我们对可能出现的结果的假设。这点要取决于我们世界观的乐观程度或悲观程度。这个也可以很快改变。

Take our child: if she is told she is 'no good' at sport, maths, singing, playing the piano or whatever, this is what her subconscious mind will believe. It will become a predominant belief for her—however erroneous that may be. Whenever an opportunity then arises to partake in the activity, she will be reluctant, shy away from trying and avoid it, because she believes she will not succeed. And that belief determines the outcome.

以儿童为例:如果在体育运动、数学、歌唱、弹钢琴或其他方面告诉小孩,她"不行",那她的潜意识里就会相信这个判断。这就会成为她心中预先设定的认识——不管错的有多离谱。不管何时有机会让她参与到这些活动中,她都会犹豫。

She has been conditioned to fail because that is what she believes. It is the truth as she sees it. It becomes a self-fulfilling prophesy.

她已经被调到了失败模式。因为她的相信,失败成了自证其源的事实。

Just as with our habits, attitudes to life, beliefs about possibilities and expectations about results are all established early on and are built on as we grow.

就像习惯一样,对人生的态度,对可能性的信仰和对结果的期待都是在早期建立的,在成长过程中固化的。

Nothing has a stronger influence psychologically on their environment and especially on their children than the unlived life of the parent.
Carl Jung

> 父母不愉快的经历对他们的环境，尤其是他们的孩子精神上的影响远大于任何其他东西。
> 卡尔荣格

If we as parents are pessimistic or cynical about the world, fearful about trying anything lest we fail, closed about our environment and the different ways people lead their lives, always expecting the worst, we can expect these to become the attitudes, beliefs and expectations of our children.

作为父母，如果我们悲观厌世，不敢做任何尝试担心失败，固步自封，从不盼好，自然而然这些态度、信仰、期待就成了孩子的。

Allow children the opportunity to control their own stories by giving them plenty of scope for stimulating their imagination by creating opportunities for them to try new things. Be gentle with their ideas. Allow and encourage them to dream big thoughts.

让孩子们有机会管控自己的事情，给予他们充分的空间，创造机会让他们尝试新东西，刺激他们的想象力。对他们的想法温柔以待。允许并鼓励他们放手去想象。

> *I have spread my dreams under your feet;*
> *Tread softly because you tread upon my dreams.*
> **WB Yeats**

在你的脚下我展开梦想的翅膀;
用你的脚轻拂,因为你踩踏的是我的梦想。
叶芝

Encourage them to persevere when they don't immediately succeed to develop resilience in a positive environment. Guide them gently along the way, at their request. Celebrate their successes.

如果在积极乐观的环境中小孩子没有即刻发展出韧性的话,鼓励他们坚持下去。温柔的引导他们,在他们的要求之下。然后取得成功的时候庆祝。

Never, ever, ever accept that a child is a lost cause. They all have many abilities and talents. It is just a question of finding which ones they enjoy best, encouraging them with a wide range of options and helping their development.

千万千万千万不要觉得一个孩子无药可救。所有小孩都有能力有天赋。问题只是在于找到他们的兴趣点,鼓励他们,给予多样的选择,帮助他们发展。

Take, for example, the case of the youngster with the turbulent childhood whose school reports were damning—'certainly on the road to failure … hopeless … rather a clown in class … wasting other pupils' time.' He was then looked after by his uncle and aunt who encouraged him to read short stories, stimulated his interest in crossword puzzles and music, bought him a mouth organ, gave him a loving home. That was John Lennon.

举个例子,年轻人有着痛苦的童年,学校的评语是:"注定走上失败的道路……没有希望……全然是班上的小丑……浪费其他学生的时间"。之后,这么一个孩子被叔叔婶婶带大,鼓励他读短的故事书,用紫米游戏和音乐刺激他的兴趣点,给他买了口琴,和充满爱的家庭。这样造就了约翰·列侬。

Or consider the case of the self-taught high school dropout, considered 'lazy, slow and dreamy', who failed the entrance exam to the Swiss Federal Polytechnic in Zurich, failed to reach the required standard in most subjects other than physics and maths, where he was encouraged, stimulated and inspired by perceptive and caring teachers. That was Albert Einstein.

再来看个例子:他高中辍学,自学成才,老师评语 " 懒惰、慢、 不现实",瑞士联邦科技大学入学考试失败,除了物理和数学其他科目都没有达标,但在慧眼识才的导师的关爱和鼓 励下不断成长 。这个人就是阿尔伯特 ·爱因斯坦。

How about the case of the high school student judged by his teachers to be 'turbulent, quarrelsome, disobedient and unbearable' until given clear responsibility and encouragement in the army. That was Charles de Gaulle.

再以高中时候被老师判断为:"叛逆、好争斗、不听话、无法忍受",但在军中被赋予了具体的指责和鼓励的查尔斯·戴高乐。

And what about Winston Churchill, who had an unhappy childhood, a poor relationship with his father, was the pupil with the lowest grades in the lowest class, left school early and only passed the exams to the Royal Military College at the third attempt.

温斯顿·丘吉尔又何尝不是如此。童年不幸,恶劣的父子 关系,差班成绩最差的学生,早早离开学校,第三次才考上皇家军事大学。

He was recognized there as being very bright, having exceptional courage, great English language and oratorical skills, enormous energy and considerable strength of purpose. He went on to be voted one of the greatest Britons of all time.

在军校,大家认为他聪明、过人的勇气,英语优秀,口才一流,精力充沛,目标明确。曾被选为最伟大的英国人。

As our case studies grew into adults and were helped to acquire and respond to responsibility, they decided on their own careers. Some did so by the force of their personalities, but most were allowed and encouraged in their vocations and activities by mentors and teachers.

我们的案例研究跟进到他们的成人阶段。这些习惯能帮助他们获得责任并对责任做出良好反馈，他们可以自己决定自己的职业选择。有些人是靠性格的力量，但大多数人是在导师和老师的鼓励和允许下实现的。

In the business world, it's called empowerment. It means allowing employees to be self-directed rather than instructed, motivated rather than depressed, responsible rather than dependent and enabled to grow and flourish rather than stultify.

商业环境中，这种做法叫做赋权。允许员工自己决定而非在指示下行事。鼓励员工，而非压制，赋予责任而非依赖领导，赋能而非磨灭自我。

Studies have shown conclusively that companies where employees feel engaged, that is who feel they are truly part of the organization they work in, share similar positive values, feel empowered and appreciated, are indeed statistically more successful. Hence the growing popularity of engagement studies by enlightened companies and organizations to measure this aspect, track progress and make changes where necessary.

研究表明员工参与度高的公司,真心觉得自己是公司的一部分的,分享更多积极的价值观,更感受到赋权,受到赞赏,统计数据上显示更加成功。因此,很多意识到这一点的公司和企业开始广泛采用参与度研究,来跟进进展,调整管理策略。

Employees are 'enabled' to exercise their own responsibilities and, as a result, have more success in a more harmonious environment.

员工被"赋能"后,可以执行他们自己的职责,其结果,在这种更加和谐的环境中创造更多好结果。

As they grow and develop, it is likely they will wish to leave their organization to progress their careers elsewhere.

随着员工的成长和发展,可能会想要离开公司到别的地方发展自己的事业。

Enlightened employers will recognize this as a positive thing and the result of the company's excellent mentoring in an environment that encourages personal growth.

开悟的员工会认识到,这是个很积极的事情,也是公司正确价值观的结果,塑造了一个鼓励员工成长的环境。

They will realize that the fact that their employees are sought by other companies is a reflection of their own excellence in developing talent, factors that will make the company even more desirable to the most aspiring and capable next generation of professionals, thus perpetuating a virtuous cycle!

他们会意识到,员工被其他公司追求也反映出本公司在人才发展上的成效显著和优越。相应地能够让公司成为更加吸引有为有能力的专业人士的地方,形成一个良性循环。

Here comes another essential learning opportunity:

我们在这个阶段又学到一点:

We are what we think.
Controlling our 'self-talk' is critical.

我们即自己所想。控制自己的言语是最关键的。

While we need to be careful about where our habits, attitudes, beliefs and expectations come from and who put them there, we also need to be mindful of **how we talk to ourselves**, our self-talk, which is directly related to them.

虽然我们要注意自己的习惯、心态、信仰、期待从哪里来,是谁那里习得的,也需要意识到自己如何与自己对话,这也是直接和他们有关的。

Self-talk is that little voice that is constantly chattering away inside our head. We sometimes hear it clearly and sometimes it is just mumbling away indistinctly, although we know the gist of what it is saying. Like our subconscious, it is directing our thoughts and our actions.

与自己的对话,需要时时发生在脑中。我们时常清晰地听到这个声音,有时又是朦朦胧胧的,虽然大意是明了的。就像潜意识,它直接影响到我们的思想和行为。

When we encounter something or someone, or even as we pass the time of day, our self-talk is chatting to us: 'I really like this;' 'This is so exciting!'; 'What a stupid remark!'; 'Why doesn't he move over into the slow lane?'

遇到某事或某人的时候,即使这一天这个时候已经过去,自我还是可以和自己对话:"我真的很喜欢这样;""这样很好!";"太傻了!";"他为什么不去慢车道?"

Earlier we saw how that little voice persuaded us to say something we had not intended to say. *That was our self-talk overriding our conscious mind.*

早先我们已经看到,这样的内心的声音会说服我们说出没有打算说的话。也就是我们的自我对话超越了意识。

Self-talk is our subconscious mind reflecting back to us the habits, attitudes, beliefs and expectations that we have created over our lifetime.

自我对话是我们一生形成的我们的行为、心态、信仰、期待映射在潜意识里。

Be mindful of what it is saying to you.

去感受自我对你的倾诉。

It is dictating your thoughts and your thoughts dictate your actions. Remember the following phrases: **As I think, I am. We are what we think. Our intentions determine our future.**

"自我"在指导你的思想,你的思想又指导着自己的行为。 记住下面这句话:我思,故我在。我们是自己思想的产 物。我们的目的决定了自己的未来。

If we think negative thoughts, that's how we'll be. If we believe the world is an inimical place, we'll be miserable. If we think the world owes us a living, we'll simply complain when we don't get our way. If we complain, we are in effect blaming others for our predicament.

如果我们有负面的消息，我们就会向着这个思想发展。如果我们相信世界是充满敌意的，我们必定痛苦不堪。如果我们认为世界欠我们的，那么在不如人意的时候必定抱怨。如果只会抱怨，我们只会把自己的窘境归咎于他人。

If we think everyone else is to blame for our misfortune, we will shift responsibility to 'others', whoever these others may be and sit back and do nothing. The negative spiral will continue unchecked. This is negative energy and we lose inner strength and power every time.

如果觉得自己的不幸都能够责怪到别人头上，那我们还是在把责任转嫁给"他人"，不管这个他人是谁，即使他什么也没做。这种负面的循环思维不加以控制会持续不断。这种负面的能量会让我们失去内在动力。

If, on the other hand, we believe that it is possible to succeed, that we can take actions to improve any given situation, that we are positive and optimistic about outcomes and are thus open to solutions, that is how we will behave. If we believe that, for every situation we encounter, there is positive learning to be gained and a thoughtful and loving response to be given, then we create positive energy and we gain inner strength and power.

如果说，我们相信有成功的可能，如果付诸行动，改善现状就有成功的可能，这样的正面乐观的对结果的预期就能带来开放的解决方案，也影响我们的行为。如果我们相信，自己遇到的每个情势下，都有积极的办法可以学习，思虑周全和关爱的反馈，那么我们就能创造正面的能量，获得内在动力和力量。

Whenever we feel a little down or uncomfortable or unhappy about something, there is a reason. We need to examine that reason carefully in order to find the right response and gain benefit rather than the opposite.

感觉低落的时候，不舒服的时候，不开心的时候，总是有个原因的。我们需要仔细地检视原因，找到正确的应对方式，从而获得有益的结果而非反之。

Suppose we have just been with friends in a social situation, and we come away feeling a little negative, we have to ask ourselves very honestly and dispassionately why. Was it something someone said or did that made us feel inadequate, angry, overlooked, silly, aggrieved, resentful or belittled? Was it that we made a comment we felt was important but was dismissed? Was it how we were 'judged' by our friends?

假设我们和朋友在社交场景中共处，自己开始有负面的情感，那就得问问自己为什么。是因为谁说了还是做了什么让自己感觉不足、愤怒、被忽视、觉得自己傻、难过、怨恨还是被贬低？是因为别人评价了我们认为重要的东西？是因为被朋友批评了？

Close and careful examination of these emotions will lead us to discover what it was that triggered our negative response. When we discover what it was, and, say, we conclude that we heard a comment that we felt dismissed something we had said without any consideration, we discover that our discomfort is the result of feeling resentful about having been ignored.

近距离仔细地审视这些情绪能让我们发现其中的内涵，是什么导致了我们的负面反应。发现了之后，比如我们确定了是因为听到了别人的评语让自己很难过，因为自己说话时考虑不周全，那就明白了是这种忿恨被忽视了导致的。

What should our reaction be?

之后该怎么做呢？

On the one hand, we can continue to feel aggrieved and unhappy, resentful, disappointed, even angry and vengeful. 'How could my friend have so dismissed me?' 'What sort of a friend would do this?' 'This can't be a true friend.' 'We're clearly very different.' 'Maybe I should drop this friendship?'

一方面，我们持续感觉悲痛不开心、愠怒、失望，甚至愤怒，想报复。"为什么我的朋友要怼我？""什么朋友才会这样对待别人？""肯定不是真朋友。""我们道不同不相为谋。""这种朋友是不是该断交了？"

Or we can learn from this, and all future encounters, by asking ourselves what would be a wiser, more mature, more loving response, rather than our automatic, angry one. Is our friend not entitled to her views, even negative ones? Could we have expressed the thought differently? Or maybe not at all? Isn't our friendship greater than this? Have I not done exactly the same thing on other occasions? Maybe this wasn't the right occasion anyway to introduce this thought? Is it heathy to maintain this negative energy? And for what purpose? Who really cares other than me? Is it good to allow our perception of the motives or actions of others to control our emotions?

我们也可以从中学习到，未来所有的类似情况的解决办法，问问自己有没有更智慧、更成熟、更有爱的回复，而不是不假思索的、愤怒的回复。是我们的朋友没有权利持有自己的视角，即使是负面的视角？我们可不可以换个办法表达想法？或者根本不说？我们的友情是不是比这个更重要？我是不是在别的情境下也做过类似的事情？也许这个想法不该在这个场景里提及？保持这种负面能量健康吗？有什么目的？除了我谁会这么想？用我们的角度来判断他人的动机或者行为正确吗？

Forgiving is a much more positive force for happiness. Letting go is so much more relieving. Both of these enhance our inner strength.

原谅是走向幸福的积极力量。放手也如此的释然。这两者都能强化我们的内在力量。

Viewing occasions when we feel low with a response based on wisdom and compassion rather than anger and hurt creates much more positive energy and happiness.

感觉低落的时候审视当下的场景,用智慧和同情心来做出反应,而非愤怒和伤人的心,这样做能创造更多的正能量和快乐。

Which response would we rather have?

我们应当怎样回复?

If we can make this response a behaviour that is second nature to us, it will lead to the right response and the right action. The right action will lead to a commitment to view life and our universe in a different and more positive way, and commitment will lead to transformed results.

如果我们把这种回复建立成一种行为机制,成了我们的第二天性,就会带来正确的反应和正确的行动。正

确 的反应会带来正确认识人生和宇宙的承诺,用一种不同的,正向的方法。这种态度会转换成结果。

***Until one is committed, there is hesitancy,
the chance to draw back, always
ineffectiveness. Concerning all acts of
initiative (or creation),
there is one elementary truth,
the ignorance of which kills countless
ideas and splendid plans:
that the moment one definitely commits
oneself, then Providence moves too.***
W H Murray

在确认前,总是有犹豫,也有可能撤回,
总是有无效的机会。对所有的事情担心,
又一个根本的 真相,就是忽视了扼杀了无数新想法和
精彩的计划:这个时刻自己会到来。
天意会到。

It is remarkable how success breeds success, as long as we have the persistence, resilience and commitment to take appropriate and wise action, not blindly but in an attitude of openness to constructive suggestions.

成功带来成功,这点让人惊讶不已,只要我们持之以恒、不畏挫折、专注于适合的、明智的行动,而不盲目,秉持开放的态度接受建设性的建议。

Using imagination to change the picture

用想象力助力改变

What to do if you catch your self-talk muttering negative thoughts:

万一发现自己和自己对话开始出现负面思想怎么办呢?

1. **Stop the negative thought right there!**
1. 马上停止负面想法!

2. **Confront your thought directly.**
2. 直面你的思想。

3. **Make the decision to alter it and use your imagination to change the picture.**
3. 下定决心做出改变,用想象力做出改变。

Consider the following: the cyclist is riding too slowly ahead of you and you're in your car becoming increasingly frustrated because you can't overtake (but might be tempted to with dangerous consequences).

试想一下,你的车前面有一个骑自行车的人,骑得太慢。你坐在车里越来越郁闷,自己无法超车(但是又很想,然而心里知道可能后果很危险)。

Your self-talk becomes negative and says to you: 'Why can't he move over or speed up?'; 'Why can't he just steer into the side so I can get by?'; 'Cyclists are such a menace;' 'He's holding up the entire traffic!'

你的自我对话变得负面,开始对自己说:"为什么他就不能一边去,要么就骑快一点?";"干嘛不能挪到旁边去,我好超车?";"骑自行车的人简直就是噩梦;""他这是占着道!"

Now, stop the negative thoughts dead!

现在,停止这种负面的想法!

Use your imagination to change the picture by visualizing something different and more positive.

用自己的想象力改变这个画面,设想一个不同而又正面的景象。

For example, in the case of being slowed down by the cyclist, change the picture and **visualize this instead: that cyclist could be my son, my daughter or my friend.**

例如:因为骑车的人而减速,试试这么想:骑车这个人可能是我的儿子,我的女儿或者朋友。

Say to yourself: 'As a responsible, loving and moral person, my duty is to protect them absolutely.'

对自己说:"作为一个理性的、有爱的、有道德的人,我的责任是保护他们。"

If it were my own child on the bike, my self-talk would be very different and so would my behaviour and actions.

如果骑车的这个人是我自己的孩子,我会对自己说一番完全不同的话,我的行为和行动也会完全不同。

By changing the picture, my self-talk shifts from a negative, irritated, potentially dangerous attitude, to one that is more caring and patient—and a lot safer. If I do this each time I am confronted with such a situation, my anxiety reduces and I behave in a calmer, more considered manner. By taking decisions and making choices based on wisdom and love, rather than anger and resentment, I gain inner strength. The more I do this, the easier it gets and, in time, it becomes second nature and a much happier way to live.

通过改变这个画面,把自我对话从负面、令人反感,可能带来危险心态,向更加关爱、有耐性,更加安全的方 向转变。如果每次遇到这样的情形,都这样处理的话, 我的焦虑也会减少,行事更平和,考虑更周全。用智慧和爱为基础去做决策做选择，而不是只听从愤怒和怨恨，我获得了内心的力量。越这样做，越容易。总有一刻，会变成第二天性，也是一个更让人幸福的生活方式。

This essentially Stoic method applies to any of our anxieties, stresses and fears and works equally well with all of them.

这本质上是斯多葛学派的法则，应用到了解决焦虑、压力、恐惧的问题中，效果也都很好。

It is a form of exposure therapy. which is arguably the best scientifically supported technique in psychotherapy.

这是一种暴露式的治疗方法，也是心理治疗中被证明最科学的技巧。

It takes some practice and repetition. Exercise by observing behaviour first in mildly stressful situations and deliberately alter the picture. The more we practise, the easier it becomes and positive results will inevitably follow.

这需要反复的练习和重复。练习包括现在中等压力的环境下观察行为，有意识地转换画面。越练习，越容易形成，积极的结果也随之而来。

We can create a new, healthier, safer, calmer habit.

我们可以创造一个新的、更健康更安全更平和的习惯。

__Take away thy opinion, and then there is taken away the complaint, "I have been harmed." Take away the complaint "I have been harmed," and the harm is taken away.__
Marcus Aurelius

移除你的观念，把抱怨拿走，"我受到伤害了。"拿走抱怨"我受到伤害了，"伤害就被拿走了。
马可·奥勒留

Overriding our self-talk and changing the picture is relevant also to collective environments, where group dynamics take over and collective lemming-like behaviours then occur.

覆盖自我的对话，改变画面这样也和集体的环境相关。团体的动态替代了集体从众无脑的行为。

Collective self-talk, as in a business or any wider environment, is called rumour or post-truth. This can be highly damaging as it promulgates falsehoods and stimulates individual untruthful self-talk and all the emotions that go with that.

集体的自我对话,就像在商业环境或者更广泛的环境中,被称作谣言,或者后真相。因为它本身会传播假性的内容,刺激个体不真实的自我对话和相应的情绪,所以破坏性很大。

When situations are ambiguous or uncertain and there is an absence of official information or fact, people make it up—they invent the 'facts'. And they will usually make them up negatively. The really bad news is that life is always ambiguous, so we are constantly bombarded by half-truths and opinion masquerading as fact.

情况变得模糊或者不确定的时候,就会感觉缺失一种官方信息,或者事实,于是大家就开始编故事——发明"事实"。而发明出来的"事实"往往是负面的。实际最不妙的问题是:人生其实总是模糊的,因为我们总是不断地被半真半假的信息和被别人的想法打扮过的信息充斥着。

Everything we hear is an opinion, not a fact.
Everything we see is a perspective, not the truth.

我们听到的一切都只是观点,而非事实。我们看到的一切都只是视角,而非真相。

Because all is opinion, everything
is what you suppose it to be.
Marcus Aurelius

> 因为一切只是观点，一切只是你该看到的。
> 马可·奥勒留

The only way to counter this negativity is to avoid believing rumours—or, worse still, condoning or agreeing with them—until we know the facts.

唯一能够对抗这种负面的办法是避免相信谣言，或者，谴责或同意，直到找到真相。

In the same way that we need to question our self-talk and override it when it is clearly pointing in the wrong direction, so too we have to recognize when rumour is simply collective self-talk and not based on factual information.

也可以用这种办法质疑自己的的对话，如果明显指向错误结论的话，可以用这个方法覆盖与自己的对话，当然我们也要认识到，谣言只是自我对话的集合体，并非是事实性信息。

Our self-talk, like collective self-talk, reflects all the prejudices we have acquired. Be mindful of that. Listen carefully to what you're saying to yourself. Then change the picture if it isn't what you want.

我们的自我对话，就像自我对话，反映出了我们所有的骄傲。心里要记得这一点。仔细的倾听自己所说的。然后，如果不是自己想要的画面，就改变。

Remember too that it is not the event or person that is the cause of our anxiety or frustration, it is the view we ourselves are taking of them, the view that our self-talk is expressing, that is causing the problem.

同时也不要忘记并非事件或人本身是我们焦虑和挫折的根源,而是我们看待自身的观点导致的。是我们自我对话所表达的,导致了问题。

Man is disturbed not by things, but by the views he takes of them.
Epictetus

人不以物分类,而以观点分类。
埃皮克提图

When we allow ourselves to be irritated, angry or anxious about events or people, we need to remember that it is not the event itself or the person that is the irritant—they are either neutral or totally indifferent—it is **our own internal image, our own judgment**, that is the cause. If we change the internal picture, our judgment will change too.

一旦允许自己被某些事件或者人刺激到、放任自己生气或者焦虑,我们就要记得,并非事件本身或这些人让我们烦。他们都是中性或者完全无关的,是我们内在的影响,我们自己的判断,才是真正的根源。只要改变内在的画面,我们的判断就会随之而变。

*If you are pained by external things,
it is not they that disturb you,
but your own judgment of them. And it is in
your power to wipe out that judgment now.*
Marcus Aurelius

如果外在的东西给我们带来痛苦,
那痛苦并非来自外在,而是你自身对外在的评判。
你有能力擦掉这些评判。
马可·奥勒留

How often have we pre-judged someone, believing them to be boring or obnoxious, only to find, when we get to know them, that they are anything but our previous assumption of them? We created a view in our mind that was completely false and it had disturbed us quite unnecessarily.

我们是否经常预先拼盘某人,相信他们很无聊或者很讨厌,之后,等我们开始了解他们的时候,才发现,他们根本不是我们预想的那样,甚至相去甚远?我们在自己内心里创造了一种观点,一种完完全全错误的观点,这种观点也非常没有必要地扰乱了我们。

Had we started out with a more open mind and not allowed our *pre*-judgment, or prejudice, to dictate our self-talk, we would have discovered the positives sooner.

如果一开始以一种开放的心态，不让我们的预制判断或者偏见，左右了我们的自我对话，我们就能更早的发现正面的信息。

How many other times have we allowed our prejudices to limit our enjoyment of the world and our happiness?

还有多少次我们纵容自己的偏见限制了自己享受这个世界，限制了自己的幸福？

'An unexamined life is not worth living,' said Socrates and Plato believed that happiness comes from taking positive, moral decisions and actions.

"没有经过审慎的人生是不值得的。"苏格拉底这么说道，柏拉图相信幸福来自乐观的心态、道德的决定和行为。

Learning to control our self-talk is key to ***examining*** our mind, creating more positive pictures, adjusting our viewpoint and stimulating the opportunity for happiness.

学会控制我们的自我对话，是审视自己思想，创造更加乐观积极的画面，调整自己的观点，激活走向幸福的机会的关键。

Use a quiet moment to stop and **listen** to what your self-talk is saying to you. Is it positive or negative, sarcastic or complimentary, uplifting or depressing, reasonable or excessive? See if you can detect a pattern.

花片刻时间静静地停下来听自己的声音。是积极乐观还是负面悲观,是讽刺还是赞美,是提振士气还是压抑抑郁,是理性还是过分?看看能不能察觉到自己的模式。

If you are not satisfied with what you find, catch your unsatisfactory self-talk next time it arises and make a clear effort to **stop and change it right there**. Replace the negative self-talk with a more positive image and create a new self-talk for yourself.

假设你对自己的发现不满意,下次在这个令人不满意的自我对话出现时,抓住它,明确地做出努力停止然后立刻做出改变。把这种负面的自我对话换成积极的图像,为自己创造新的对话。

Consider the following case: Mrs G would frequently burst into tears on routine occasions such as walking the dogs in the park, on shopping trips, or at home in the kitchen or even at dinner parties. She was deeply unhappy, verging on depression.

试想一下:G夫人市场因为一些日常的事情,比如带狗到公园散步,出门买东西,在家里厨房里或者晚餐会的时候痛哭流涕。内心深处,她非常不愉快,几近抑郁。

When asked why, she said she was still in mourning for her mother. When asked how long ago her mother had died, she said some five years before.

问她为什么,她回答说她还在悼念自己的母亲。问她母亲离世多久了,她说大约五年多前了。

What was happening was that when, for example, she took the dogs for a walk in the park, something she used to enjoy doing with her mother, a picture of her mother during her last days would spring up in her mind and she would immediately become very sad, leading to floods of tears.

到底是什么让她难过呢?比如:带狗到公园散步,以前喜欢和母亲一起做的事情,和母亲最后的日子的画面浮现出来,她立刻就会难过,涌出泪水。

She loved her mother very much and quite understandably missed her.

G夫人很爱她的母亲,思念母亲合情合理。

In order to start to address the issue, she was asked to take time, at home and on regular occasions to ***visualize*** her mother, not in her last days but when she was healthy and full of life and to ***picture*** her happy, laughing and smiling in different situations, especially those special occasions when they were together.

然而，要解决这个问题，她需要花时间，在家常规的想起自己母亲，不是去想她最后的日子，而是回想她还健康，充满生气的时候，描绘出她在不同情景下开心、开怀大笑，微笑的状态，特别是一起度过的特殊时刻。

She was asked to do this several times a day and to *look up* while doing so. (It is much more difficult to be sad when looking up.)

这个训练G夫人被要求一天多次进行，同时不断地向上看。(向上看着的时候很难悲伤起来。)

After a relatively few days, Mrs G said she was feeling much better and after three weeks her unhappiness had dissipated altogether. She still had feelings of sadness, but these were increasingly being replaced with images of happiness.

几天之后，G夫人说她感觉好些了，三个礼拜之后，她的伤感情绪渐尖消散殆尽。她还是会难过，但逐渐被幸福的画面替代。

Reflect regularly on your habits, attitudes, beliefs and expectations. Where did they come from? Who put the ideas there in the first place and are they the right ones for you? Or are they limiting your ability to move forward? Are they creating a prison for you?

反思一下自己的行为、心态、信仰和期待。都是从哪里来的。是谁先置入了这些想法,这些想法适合你吗?抑或在限制你向前的能力?是否为你建造了个监狱?

The key to our prison is in our own pocket. We have the power and freedom to open it anytime—if we so choose.

打开这个监狱的钥匙就在我们自己的口袋里。我们有能力也有自由随时解锁,只要你自己愿意。

We do not need to become chained in Plato's 'cave' unable to perceive a better life, only seeing the shadows not reality and condemned to confuse ill-considered beliefs with truth.

我们不需要被锁在柏拉图的"洞穴"中,不去想象更好的生活,只是看见影子而非真实,无法区分歪曲的信仰和真相。

Let us have the courage to escape from our prison cave!

让我们鼓起勇气从这个束缚自己的洞穴中逃出来吧!

Only then can we be in a position to climb up the stairway.

只有这样我们才能站到爬上阶梯的位置。

The secret of happiness is freedom. And the secret to freedom is courage.

通向幸福的秘密就是自由。通向自由的秘密是勇气。

THE SECOND STEP:
THE HAPPINESS OF ACHIEVING
第二步：成就带来的幸福感

We have seen how instant gratification, while providing short-term and rather ephemeral happiness, can quickly become problematic if not set in a sensible context with a modicum of discipline.

我们已经看到了，虽然即使满足能够带来短暂的幸福感，但随即，如果不放在合理的场景中，不加控制，很容易带来各种问题。

Setting a sensible context is the result of considered thought combined with deliberate action to develop a new habit.

建立一个合理的场景，是深思熟虑、精心设计的结果，也是培养

Developing a new habit is an act of achievement, as opposed to self-gratification, because it requires effort and energy and, if successful, results in a sense of achievement, which is the *happiness of achieving*.

建立一种新习惯,相对即时满足来说,就是一种成就。因为这个新习惯的简历需要投入努力和精力。如果成功了,所带来的成就感,就是我们所说的成就的幸福感。

In the Stoic philosophy, the only two things we can control are our **thoughts** and **actions**. When we want or need to change a habit, we have the opportunity to control both in such a way as to improve our life and happiness.

在斯多葛学派的哲学理念里,我们唯一可以控制的两件事情就是自己的思想和行动。要改变一个习惯,我们就有了同时控制这两者的机会,并通过这样的统一改善自己的人生,获得幸福感。

Changing habits requires patience, self-awareness and some discipline, but the discipline is only required until such time as the new habit has been established—it is no longer needed once the new behaviour has become automatic. It is then much easier.

改变一个习惯,需要耐心、自知、自律。其中,自律只是在建立新习惯的时候才需要。而新的习惯一旦形成自动模式,就不再需要了。那个时候一切会变得轻松许多。

Creating a new habit can be done in the following way:

建立一个新习惯可以按照以下步骤实现:

1. The first step is to be absolutely clear **what we want to create as a new habit and why** and **write it down**. Committing to paper has the advantage that it cannot be overridden by our subconscious mind. It is there to be seen all the time, whereas just thinking ideas have no lasting value and tomorrow will be another day with another thought and no action.
1. 第一步是要绝对清楚地了解我们要形成一个什么样的习惯,为什么。把这些信息都写下来。写在纸上的好处是,写下来的东西不会被潜意识改写。写在纸上,我们随时都能看到。心里想的东西没有持续的价值,明日复明日,明日何其多。

2. The second step is to enumerate and **write down as many reasons as we can gather why we absolutely need to create this new habit**, so as to develop an **overwhelming** case to ourselves that **such a change will be beneficial to us and in our own interest**.
2. 第二步要写下尽可能多的理由来说明这个新习惯必要性。给自己制造一种紧迫感,让我们清楚的看到这个改变的必要性和对自己的益处。

3. The third step is to write or rewrite our new habit **in the present tense and in the affirmative** (no negatives as the subconscious mind, as we now know, cannot process a negative). The fact that it is in the present tense creates a dissonance with the subconscious mind (which says it isn't true) thus creating an energy to either do something to reconcile the new habit with a new reality or go back to the old reality. We also need to **visualize ourselves in the new habit,** remembering the formula I + V x R = NR (Imagination + Visualisation x Repetition = New Reality).

3. 第三步就是把新的习惯写下来,用现在时(英语语法时态)并用加强语气写下来(因为我们知道,潜意识时无法处理否定的信息的)。用现在时写的好处是能够给潜意识制造一种不适感(因为潜意识知道,"现在"的习惯不是这样的)。如此一来,潜意识就得做点什么,要么制造一个新的现实与这个新习惯和解,要么退回到过去的现实。我们也可以对新习惯进行视觉化。记得这个等式I + V x R = NR (想象+视觉化x重复=新的现实)。

4. The fourth is to **begin immediately** (not tomorrow or next time we have a moment) and read our new commitment morning, noon and night and whenever we feel the need to keep strong (notice the absence of any negative

notions of giving up or finding it hard to find the time). If we can, we should link this to a program of short-term goals.

4. 第四步:立刻开始(不要等到明天或者下次)在早上、中午、晚上,或者任何一个我们觉得需要强化这个新习惯的时候,把自己的承诺读出来。(注意我们没有用任何负面的,比如"放弃","很难找到时间"等这类表达)如果可以的话,把这个承诺/计划和一个短期目标关联起来。

5. The fifth is to **persevere** and maintain steady progress until the new habit has become second nature, whereupon it ceases to become an effort as the subconscious mind reconciles the dissonance and adopts the new state.
5. 第五步则是保持稳定的进步,直到新习惯成为了自己的第二天性,不再需要"努力",也不再会有潜意识与现实之间的不适感。

Let's take an example.

举个例子吧。

George is a middle-aged man who has done little exercise in the past twenty years, is overweight, unfit, with high blood pressure and an unhealthy body mass index. He works hard and as soon as he gets home he pours himself a drink, has a meal with a glass (or two) of wine and sits himself in front of the TV until it's time to go to bed, which he does at approximately the same time every weekday.

乔治是一个中年人。过去20年来很少做体育运动,此时此刻的他胖了,没有线条,还有高血压,BMI各项指标也不正常。乔治工作很努力,但一回到家,就想喝一杯。吃个饭喝一两杯红酒,看一会儿电视,就该睡觉了。每个工作日基本如此,连时间点都一样。

George would like to do something about this—not least because his medical was rather alarming and his metabolic age was significantly higher than his actual age.

乔治想做出改变,不单是因为健康在敲警钟,他的新陈代谢也较同龄人缓慢。

Let's follow the steps.

于是他按照下面的步骤:

1. Be clear about the new habit we want to create and why, and then write it down. After a few attempts, George writes: 'I want to be fit in order to be healthy.'
1. 绝对清楚地了解我们要形成一个什么样的习惯,为什么。把这些信息都写下来。尝试几次之后,乔治写到:"我想变得有型,这样更健康。"

2. Write down as many reasons as possible why this is vital and in our own interest, and create an overwhelming case for change. George writes dozens of reasons, including: 'I want to see my children (and grandchildren) grow up;' 'I want to feel good about myself;' 'I want to feel alive;' 'I want to feel happy;' 'I want to have more energy;' 'I want to enjoy playing football with my son;' 'I want to be comfortable running a half marathon;' 'I want my family to be proud of me;' 'I want to show myself that I can achieve difficult things;' 'And if I don't change, my health, my family, my prospects, my enjoyment of life, my happiness and those of my nearest and dearest will be unhappily affected.'

2. 写下尽可能多的理由来说明这个新习惯必要性。给自己制造一种紧迫感,让我们清楚的看到这个改变的必要性和对自己的益处。乔治写了数十个理由,比如:"我想看着自己的孩子(孙子孙女)长大";"我想要良好的自我感觉";"我想感受活力";"我想要快乐";"我想精力充沛";"我想和儿子一起踢足球";"我想要轻轻松松跑个半程马拉松";"我希望家人为我骄傲";"我想向自己证明我能做到";"如果我再不改变,我的健康,我的家人,我的未来,我的人生的乐趣,我的幸福,我最亲近、最爱的人都会被影响到。"

3. Write our new habit in the present tense and in the affirmative. George writes: 'I AM A FIT

AND HEALTHY PERSON!' 'But you're not,' says the subconscious mind, 'so stop messing around and come back to the person you really are!' This is why George's reasons for changing have to be well thought through and persuasive and where visualizing the new state comes in: 'I AM A FIT AND HEALTHY PERSON and, what's more, I can see exactly how I look and feel as a fit, healthy person. That is who I really am.'

3. 把新的习惯写下来，用现在时和加强语气写下来。乔治写到："我是一个有型又健康的人！"，"但你不是啊"，潜意识这个时候跳出来说，"所以就不要忙活了，做回你自己！" 就是因为这个，所以乔治要做出改变的理由应该是经过深思熟虑的，而且要有说服力，并用视觉化把新的状态建立起来。比如，告诉自己："我很有型，很健康。不止如此，我能想象出自己变得有型、健康以后的样子。那个才是我真正的样子。"

4. George reads his statement of commitment several times a day, schedules a program of exercise on a regular basis, signs up with a personal trainer to start off, has a program of short- and longer-term goals, finds time to exercise during lunch breaks, in the evening after work, before going to work and at weekends, reduces his alcohol consumption to weekends only, reduces his portion sizes and switches to a healthier, reduced-sugar diet.

4. 乔治把自己的承诺每天都读上几遍,做了个锻炼计划,请了私人教练,制定了短期和长期目标。他在中饭的时候找机会锻炼,晚上下班后,上班前,周末休息的时候找机会锻炼。减少酒精的摄入,仅在周末饮酒,并用更健康、少糖的饮料替代。

5. After three months, George is still reading his statement of commitment every day and evening and his progress has been very rapid. He goes regularly to the gym and has had to increase his goals several times as they have mostly been achieved. He enjoys playing football with his son and is much better able to do so as he has more energy and enthusiasm. He is happier at work and at home, has lost weight, his blood pressure is closer to normal. He now experiences what he calls a *joie de vivre*, the happiness to be alive, and he feels good about himself. Above all, the new routine seems now to be quite easy and has become a way of life for him. He has no intention of going back.

5. 三个月后,乔治还是会每天早晚读一下自己的承诺。他进步很快。锻炼很规律。因为之前的目标都完成的很顺利,乔治还不断给自己增加了难度。他很喜欢和儿子一起踢球。特别是精力更充沛,踢起球来也更有激情。他在公司也好,在家也好,都比以前更开心。体重降了下来,血压也接近正常。用他自己的话说,现在就有一种joie de vivre——活着的幸福感。现在他自我感觉很好。更 重要的是,新的习惯已经自然而然成了他生活的 一部分。他不会再回到过去了。

George will need to continue to exercise for the rest of his life and may need to enlist the help of a personal trainer from time to time to maintain his enthusiasm and learn new methods.

乔治可能一生都要坚持锻炼,偶尔还是需要私人教练的帮助,维持运动激情,打破训练瓶颈。

He has, however, experienced the happiness of achieving.

但是,乔治体验到了成就带来的幸福感。

George is a hypothetical example. He is, however, one that is rooted in real situations and real outcomes, which happen every day.

乔治是一个假想的例子。但是,他的情况和结果每天都在上演。

Keeping physically fit is of course also a wonderful way of feeling happy, not so much because of the adrenaline rush (although that's nice too) but because being fit and healthy allows us to feel good about ourselves, allows us to view life more positively, is better for our health, gives us greater optimism and helps us to see our universe more benignly.

保持体格有型是实现自我感觉愉悦的好方法，不单是因为肾上腺素（虽然这个时候感觉确实良好），而是因为有型和健康能让我们自我感觉良好，让人更积极地看待人生。对健康有益，让人更乐观，让我们用更善意的眼光看到这个宇宙。

The methodology described above is applicable to any and all circumstances where change is wanted and a new habit is desired.

上面提到的方法，可以适用于任何情况、任何问题，只要是需要做出改变，建立新习惯。

Look well into thyself; there is a source of strength which will always spring up if thou wilt always look.

到你的内心去寻找；只要你去找，
永远都有一股力量，随时为你爆发。

The happiness of achieving comes about from doing something that requires effort and energy, presents a challenge (however small) and can be shown to have been achieved when completed.

成就带来的幸福感在于付出努力和精力达成的目标。不论这个挑战有多小,完成的时候都是一种成就

One of the ways of re-establishing confidence in someone who has suffered psychological trauma is to allow them to set small goals for themselves related to the re-establishment of trust not only in themselves but also in others, and that they can achieve.

帮助心理受创的人重建自信的一个办法,就是让他们为自己和他人,设定一些与重建信任相关的小目标。

In our busy lives, how often do we set out to do any number of things, make arrangements with friends and family, take care of myriad domestic, financial and social imperatives only to find, by the end of the day, we have only done a fraction of them?

你是不是也有这样的经历,常常列出了一堆待办清单,和家人朋友做了各种安排,处理家庭、财务、社交要务。最后却发现,我们的计划只完成了一些边角。

We then feel both guilty and bad, and promise to correct this pattern of behaviour, only to do it all over again.

我们又因此感觉内疚、自责,决心打破这个行为模式。最后却发现再来一次结果还是一样。

If we ask people, 'How often, on average, do you only speak the truth?' most people will score well above eighty percent and they will be truthful in their answer.

如果你问一个人,"平均来说,你多久说一次真话?"大多数人的回答是八成以上。这是真话。

If we now ask them, 'How often do you keep your promises?' the response is much lower.

现在如果你问:"你承诺的事有多少做到了?"答案肯定不如前一个肯定。

Promises are, or should be, a **commitment to achieve** with and for ourselves or with and for another. To the extent that we honour our commitment, we feel a sense of satisfaction and happiness. To the extent that we fail to meet that commitment, not only do we feel unhappy, we have also psychologically damaged our self-esteem and we lose inner strength.

承诺的事情应当是决心为自己或他人完成的。完成自己的承诺,能给人一种满足感和幸福感。如果未能完成 承诺,我们不但会闷闷不乐,还可能伤害自己的自尊心,失去内在力量。

***Always bear in mind that your own
resolution to succeed is more important
than any other one thing.***
Abraham Lincoln

永远都要记得,你自己对成功的承诺,
比任何其他事情都重要。
亚伯拉罕·林肯

The importance of self esteem

自尊的重要性

People with high self-esteem will on average always perform better than people with low self-esteem. Poor self-esteem leads to poor or even negative performance and we are back in the vicious cycle of a bad habit perpetuating itself.

总体来看,自尊心强的人要比自尊心弱的人表现的更好。自尊心弱会使人表现欠佳,甚至带来负面影响。最后我们又会回到坏习惯的恶性循环中。

We need to convert the vicious cycle into a virtuous one.

我们要把这个恶性循环转变为良性循环。

One of the best ways to increase self-esteem is to achieve predetermined goals that have some appropriate level of challenge.

增强自尊心,有很多好办法,其中一个就是实现具有一定挑战性的预定目标。

By nature, human beings are motivated by goals and this creates energy and enthusiasm for their completion. Goal-setting is also vital for survival and studies have shown that people in retirement who have goals have a longer life expectancy than those who haven't.

天性使然,人类会受到目标的激励而前行,这种机制为目标的最终完成创造出能量和热情。目标设定同样对人类的生存至关重要,研究表明退休后依然有目标的人要比没有目标的人拥有更长的预期寿命。

At the same time, we need to be mindful of setting goals that are our own, not those defined by others.

同时,要注意,我们设定的目标是自己的,不要被他人定义。

We need to take care not to 'under-live' our potential because of all the past information that has been absorbed in the expectation part of our subconscious.

还要注意，不要因为我们潜意识是通过吸收过往的信息来设定期待值，而"低估"了自己的潜力。

A good coach is one who sees more potential in an individual than that person, or indeed others, can see themselves. Let's remember the case of Helen Keller and her coach, Anne Sullivan.

一个好的老师能够从学生身上挖掘出更多的潜力，他能看到学生自己或其他人意识不到的地方。不要忘记海伦·凯勒和她的老师安·沙利文的故事。

The setting and accomplishment of goals, which is the essence of the happiness of achieving, is also the best way of moving out of instant gratification and its attendant risk of stagnation, and building self-esteem—vital to all the next steps on the stairway.

目标的设定和达成是实现幸福的本质，也是摆脱即时满足最好的办法。不但能避免即使满足所带来的停滞不前，也能帮人建立自尊心。对通往幸福阶梯的下一步至关重要。

Children, especially between the ages of five and twelve, need to win approval by demonstrating skills and abilities that are valued by their parents, peers and their environment so that they can begin to develop a sense of pride in their accomplishments, positive self-esteem and a positive self-image.

儿童，尤其是处于5岁到12岁年之间的孩子，需要向父母和自己的同龄人以及自己所处的环境所重视的技能和本领来赢得认可。通过这样的成绩来建立自豪感，并树立起积极的自尊心和正面的自我形象。

Parents need to reinforce and encourage the initiatives that children suggest and, while allowing some failures to avoid overconfidence and encourage modesty, should celebrate successes where specific skills and competences have been developed and demonstrated. This builds self-esteem.

父母应当鼓励孩子主动，并且不断强化这种习惯，同时也要允许孩子失败，避免他们过度自信。鼓励孩子谦虚行事的同时，也应该在看到他们某方面取得进步的时候庆祝他们的成果。这样做有助于帮助他们建立自尊。

If our child does not develop such skills she may begin to feel inferior, leading to low self-esteem and a lower ability to experience the happiness of achieving.

小孩子如果没有发展出这样的技能，就可能会感觉自己低人一等，自尊心下降，很难体会到取得成绩所带来的幸福感。

In order for children, and adults, to build their self-esteem, and their confidence, they need goals and the wherewithal to achieve them—ambition, determination, energy, drive, focus, resilience, hard work and competence.

要帮助儿童和成年人建立起自尊和自信,首先要设定目标,其次还需要愿心、决心、精力、动力、专注力、抗压能力、勤奋和能力等这些必要因素。

If you set yourself to your present task along the path of true reason, with all determination, vigour, and good will: if you admit no distraction, expecting nothing, shirking nothing, but self-content with each present action taken in accordance with nature and a heroic truthfulness in all that you say and mean—then you will lead a good life. And nobody is able to stop you.
Marcus Aurelius

如果你能带着决心、活力、善意,沿着真正理性的道路
去完成现定的目标;如果你全神贯注、无所期待、
无所畏惧,对自己每一个按照自然之道所作出的行为,
对自己所说所表达都如英雄般真实。那么,
你的人生就会很好。没有人能够阻止你。
马可·奥勒留

Setting goals

目标的设定

Setting goals which are then met is a valid way of building self-esteem and gaining joy from the happiness of achieving.

设定目标并最终达成目标是建立自尊和享受实现目标所带来的幸福感的有效方法。

The act of changing a habit, as we have seen, is in itself a goal achieved and the methodology has already been explained.

正如我们所看到的,改变一个习惯实际上就是一个完成目标的过程。在前面的章节中我们也讲述了实现目标的相关方法。

The wider question then arises and must be addressed: what goals should we have? How challenging should they be? How specific or vague? How many should we have? Over what time scale?

于是一个更广泛的问题便产生了:我们应该设定怎样的目标?这些目标应该具有多大的挑战性?目标要多具体或者多模糊?应该有多少个目标?应该给自己多长的时间?

What goals?

什么是目标？

So let's consider first what the goals might be.

我们先来思考下什么是目标。

It is often said that a goal or the goals should be SMART or even SMARTER, which stands for Specific (simple, sensible, significant), Measurable (meaningful, motivating), Achievable (agreed, doable), Relevant (reasonable, realistic, resourced, useful), Time bound (with agreed dates for completion), Evaluated and Reviewed.

经常听人说，设定目标要按照SMART原则（英文原意"明智的"，即具备S—具体性（简单、合理、重要）、M—可测量性（有意义、有动力）、A—可实现性（商定的、可行的）、相关性（合理、现实、资源保障、实用）、T—时限性（有商定的完成日期），几个单词的首字母缩写；或SMARTER，即在原先SMART的基础上增加了E（可评估性）和R（可审查性）。

This is perfectly sound and has been used very frequently, especially in a business environment, to establish **what** is required, **why** it is required, **who** is involved, **where** it takes place, **which** resources are needed and **when** it is to be completed.

这是个非常站得住脚的方法,也经常用到,尤其是在商业领域中,用来确定what(需要什么),why(为何需要),who(谁需要参加),where(在哪里进行),which(需要什么资源),when(什么时候能够完成)等这些关键要素的时候。

It is particularly relevant to the setting of immediate **tasks—once the overall direction of travel has been established**. The need for creative or imaginative solutions is not high (and sometimes positively discouraged) and the context is somewhat narrow.

在确定了目标的整体方向之后,用于解决眼前的任务时,SMART显得非常有效。在这个阶段,对具有创造性和富有想象力的解决方案的需求不是那么高(有时反而并不提倡),相应要考虑的场景也比较有限。

SMART's uses, then, are limited to specific actions, it doesn't answer the question about what our goals should be.

因此,"SMART"这个方法,仅限于特定的行动,并没有回答我们的"目标应该是什么"这个问题。

Establishing a bigger picture first

设定目标:首先,建立一个更大的设想

Establishing our goals is not a trivial exercise, but one that needs to be seen in a much wider context than is usually the case.

建立目标不是一件小事,而是一项需要放眼全局的工作。而这一点往往被人忽视。

If it is our ambition to be millionaires at thirty, or win an Olympic gold medal, or become prime minister or a concert pianist, this will not happen because we 'will' it to, or 'imagine' the outcome sufficiently positively. It will only happen by dint of tremendous sacrifices, hard work, tireless efforts, talent and a lot of good luck!

如果我们的目标是在三十岁时成为百万富翁,或者赢得奥运金牌,又或者成为首相或钢琴演奏家,只通过我们的意愿"我会"这样做或只是积极地"想象"这种结果,是不会实现这些目标的。只有通过巨大的牺牲、努力地工作、不懈地努力、发挥才能和足够的运气才能实现!

These sacrifices will affect not only our lives, but the lives of many others. There is no such thing as a single goal because of its ripple effect on other aspects of our life and those of others.

这些牺牲不仅会对我们自己的生活产生影响,也会影响到其他很多人的生活。没有一个目标是单一的,因为每一个单一的目标都会对我们自己与其他人的生活产生连锁反应。

And then, our ambition may not happen at all, or only in part.

然后,我们的雄心壮志可能根本就不会实现,或者只会实现一小部分。

If we have just a single, overweening idea or ambition in mind, and it fails, then we are likely to be much less well off than if we had not started. We will also feel disappointed and a failure and, should we have unwisely invested in the idea, a lot less well-off to boot.

假设我们有一个过于自负的想法或抱负,然后去尝试却失败了,我们的财富会比没有尝试这个项目的时候少得多。我们也会因此而感到失望和沮丧,心想:如果我们对这个想法没有进行明智地投资,我们的富裕程度也会大大降低。

Even if we are successful with our single-minded objective, what then? It is said that when Alexander the Great had succeeded in defeating all the kingdoms he could, he wept. There was no one else to conquer.

即使我们实现了一心想要达成的目标,那又怎样呢?据说当亚历山大大帝成功地征服了所有他能击败的王国后,他哭了。因为他没有可以再去征服的目标了。

Our success should be seen also in the context of our sacrifices. What did we miss out on while we were pursuing our goal so ardently? Did we have time for our family? Did we see our children grow up, play their matches, attend their concerts, find quality time for them? What happened to our health with all that stress? What happened to us as human beings?

面对成功的时候,我们也应当把自己所付出的牺牲考虑进去一起审视。在我们执着地追逐目标时的时候,都错过了什么?我们有时间陪伴家人吗?有没有陪伴孩子的成长,有没有看他们比赛,有没有参加他们的音乐会,有没有和家人实现高质量的陪伴?压力对我们的健康产生了什么影响?作为一个人,我们因此改变了多少?

Or have we simply left behind a string of unhappy relationships, estranged children, broken families and anxiety about the future, while our health has deteriorated?

还是说,我们在健康状况逐渐恶化的同时,留下了一连串悲伤的回忆、日渐疏远的孩子、支离破碎的家庭和对未来无穷无尽的焦虑?

If we did win an Olympic medal but can now no longer compete as age catches up, which it will inevitably do, what now? How do we conduct the rest of our lives? How do we avoid feeling a sense of depressive emptiness?

假设真的赢了奥运会金牌,但不可避免地,随着年龄的增长我们再也不能参加比赛了。这时候该怎么办?我们应该如何度过余生?我们要如何避免令人抑郁的空虚感?

True happiness is to enjoy the present, without anxious dependence upon the future, not to amuse ourselves with either hope or fears but to rest satisfied with what we have, which is sufficient, for he that is so wants nothing. The greatest blessings of mankind are within us and within our reach. A wise man is content with his lot, whatever it may be, without wishing for what he has not.

Letting go all else, cling to the following few truths. Remember that man lives only in the present. In this fleeting instant: all the rest of his life is either past and gone, or not yet revealed. This mortal life is a little thing, lived in a little corner of the earth: and little too is the longest fame to come, dependent as it is on a succession of fast-perishing little men who have no knowledge even of their own selves, much less of one long dead and gone.
Marcus Aurelius

真正的幸福是享受现在,而不是焦虑地依赖未来,不要拿希望或恐惧来消耗自己,而是对当前所拥有的一切满足。当下的一切就够了,做到这一点的人,不会再欲求别的东西。这对那些无欲无求的人来说已经足够。人类最大的幸福就藏在我们的内心,就在我们触手可及的范围内。智者满足于生活带给他的任何一切,而不是专注于自己所没有的。

抛开世俗的一切,只专注于以下真理。记住,人只活在当下。在这稍纵即逝的一瞬间,他的余生要么已经逝去,要么还未显现。凡人的生命是这尘世间微不足道的一件小事,即使是流芳百世的名声最终的归宿也是渺不足道的,因为它的传颂依赖于甚至都不了解自我的、即将逝去的一连串的小人物,更不用说一个早已亡故的人了。

马可·奥勒留

These quotations are not, as they might appear, a cynical call for inaction when confronted by impossible achievements.

这段引文并非如表面上那样,像是一种对无为愤世嫉俗的呼号。

Rather they are a call to look at who we are, our lives and our goals in a different way, with more humility and more wisdom. We need to prepare our inner selves in a way that will enable us to face any and all aspects of our external future tasks with equanimity, calm reasoning, an absence of fear and an acceptance that most aspects of life cannot be controlled.

相反,他是呼吁我们以一种更谦卑、更明智的方式来审视自我,审视我们的生活和目标。让内在的自我做好充分地准备来面对外来环境中的所有挑战,冷静思考、无所畏惧,平静的接受生活中无法改变的事实。

We need to be mindful that chance, fate or luck play a major role in our successes or failures, whatever we might wish to think, and learn to manage the two elements in our lives that are controllable, namely our thoughts and our actions and let go what we cannot control—but desperately try to—namely everything else.

我们需要牢记,机会、命运和运气在我们每一次的成功或失败中都扮演着重要的角色,无论我们希望什么,无论我们怎么想,我们都要学会管理我们生活中两个可控因素,即思考和行动,并放下那些我们虽尽力尝试却仍旧无法控制的事情-即生活中除思考和行动的其它所有事情。

Never let the future disturb you. You will meet it, if you have to, with the same weapons of reason which today arm you against the present.
Marcus Aurelius

> 不要让未来扰乱现在的你。未来会与你相遇,需要的话,带上今天武装你的理性去面对未来。
> 马可·奥勒留

Marcus Aurelius and many of his fellow Stoics were very successful people, enjoying wealth, fame, acclaim, power. Marcus Aurelius was considered one of the five greatest Roman emperors. He was a successful leader at a particularly difficult time for an embattled Rome and his greatest legacy is his writings and reflections.

马可·奥勒留和他许多斯多葛学派的同僚一样,都是非常成功的人,享有财富、名望、赞誉和权力。马可·奥勒留是罗马最伟大的五位皇帝之一。在罗马深陷战事的时代,马克·奥勒留展现出了杰出的领导才能。他留给世间最大的遗产便是他的著作和思想。

His philosophy was one of simplicity, reason, justice, self-discipline and calm.

他的哲学观点是简单、理性、公正、自律和冷静。

Epictetus, a major influence on Marcus Aurelius, was born a slave. He became disabled when his leg was deliberately broken. His passion for philosophy allowed him to get educated and he gained his freedom as a youth. He became an outstanding thinker, speaker and teacher. He lived a simple life, with few possessions, to the age of eighty. Given his origins as a slave, he was able to understand fully that since we are able uniquely to control our own thoughts, and no one can take that away, it follows that we are also uniquely responsible for our actions and should not be anxious about what is not within our power to influence.

埃皮克提图是对马可·奥勒留的思想产生重大影响的人。埃皮克提图生下来是个奴隶。后来,他的腿被人蓄意打断,成了残疾人。他对哲学的渴望支撑着他完成了学业,并在青年时获得了自由之身,成为了一名伟大的思想家、演说家、老师。埃皮克提图生活简朴,几乎没有什么财产,一直活到了八十岁。曾经作为奴隶的经历使他能够充分理解,既然我们有能力独自控制自己的思想,不让它被别人控制或窃取,那么我们也对因思想而采取的行动负有独一无二的责任,我们也不应该为那些超出能力范围的事情而感到焦虑。

If, then, the things which are independent of the will are neither good nor bad, and all things which do depend on the will are within our power, and no man can either take them from us or give them to us, if we do not choose, where is room for anxiety?
Epictetus

那么，如果那些独立于意志的东西既不是好的，也不是坏的，所有依赖于意志的东西都在我们的能力范围内，没有人能从我们这里拿走或给予，如果我们不加以选择，那焦虑的余地又在哪里呢？
埃皮克提图

They were successful precisely because their lives were founded and grounded on solid inner principles of virtue, reason, ethical training, humility, self-reflection, careful judgment, inner calm and freedom of thought.

他们之所以成功，正是因为他们的生活建立于美德、理性、修养、谦卑、自省、谨慎、冷静和思想自由等坚实的内在原则之上。

The happiness of achieving that they experienced was the result of the philosophical foundations that underlay their decisions and expectations.

他们所经历的成功的喜悦是把决策和期望建立在哲学基础上的结果。

Unless, they would say, our goals are founded on solid principles, regularly practiced so as to enable us to learn and grow, then even if we succeed with our goal, we will still be the same person as before, with all our fears and anxieties.

他们会说,除非我们的目标是建立在坚实的原则之上的,定期的实践使我们不断学习和成长;不然的话,即使最终我们达成了目标,成功了,我们依然和之前没有什么不同,依然背负着之前所有的恐惧和焦虑。

My true self is free. It cannot be contained.

真正的自我是自由的,是无法被人限制的。

With the benefit of this knowledge we can reset our goals in a different, more holistic context, recognizing that our goals are interdependent.

有了这些知识的帮助,我们就可以在不同的、更全面的背景下重新设定自己的目标,并认识到我们所有的目标都是相互依存的。

When establishing our goals, let us look at not just one aspect but many aspects of our lives, so as to establish a more balanced set.

制定目标时,我们不要只专注于生活的一个方面,应该着眼全局,从而建立起一个更平衡的整体。

What ambition do we have for our professional, family and social lives, leisure time and hobbies, holidays, our physical and mental health, and our wealth ambitions and retirement needs? It is important to make this list as extensive and relevant as possible, so as to cover all aspects of our life.

我们,对于自己的职业、家庭和社会生活、休闲时光和兴趣爱好、身心健康、财富渴望和退休生活有什么目标?这张目标清单列得尽可能的广泛和相关越好,以便涵盖我们生活中的方方面面。

1. Create a pie or bar chart that shows what an **ideal** work-life balance would be for each element you consider important to your life and happiness. Pencil in each bar the level of importance you would ideally attribute to it. This will establish the relative position of each element to each other as well as their overall importance. Consult your partner and family.
1. 创建一个饼图或柱状图,把你认为对生活的幸福至关重要的项目都列出来,并给每一项标出你理想状态下它的重要程度。用这个分值来确定每个项目之间的相对重要性,以及单个项目在整体中的重要程度。记得咨询一下自己的伴侣还有家人。

2. Do the same thing but this time pencil in each bar to the level that it **currently is**.
2. 重复以上的步骤,但这次标注出每一项在目前阶段的重要程度。

3. **Compare** the two charts to establish where the differences are.
3. 比较这两个图表，找出差异。

4. Think carefully about **which** of the differences need to be addressed and **how**.
4. 仔细考虑哪些差异点需要解决，如何解决。

We now have the basis for establishing a set of goals that correspond more exactly to what we really want and, hopefully, need in our lives. Also, by establishing several goals, if one does not work out, we have more to fall back on.

现在我们有了建立一整套目标的基础，这些目标更准确地符合我们真正所想所需。此外，通过多确立几个目标，即使一个目标没有达成，我们依然有其它的目标可以实现。

Which ones can we control ourselves? Which ones can we only partly control? And which ones are entirely outside our control? If any are completely outside our control, we should simply **let them go**.

哪些是自己完全可控的？哪些是部分可控的？哪些是完全脱离我们掌控的？如果有任何事情是完全超出了我们的控制，我们只能简单的选择放手。

Each goal then needs to be carefully assessed, written down in the detail that is necessary to ascertain when it has been achieved—what will it look like when achieved—and broken down into manageable pieces with reasonable timescales and clear actions.

每个目标都需要被仔细地评估,并写下每个细节,以确定达成的时间-目标达成后会怎样-然后用合理的时间范畴和清晰明确的行动将其分解为可管控的部分。

We need also to convert our goals into achievements. When it is our responsibility we need to learn how to take decisions wisely and in a timely manner. This requires concentration, courage and decisiveness. Hesitation is a recipe for procrastination and failure.

我们还需要把我们的目标转化为成就。当它成为我们的责任时,我们需要学习如何明智并及时地做出决定。这就需要一定的专注、勇气和果断。犹豫是拖延和失败的铺路石。

> *Concentrate on what you have to do. Fix your eyes on it. Remind yourself that your task is to be a good human being … Then do it, without hesitation, and speak the truth as you see it. But with kindness. With humility. Without hypocrisy.*
> **Marcus Aurelius**

> 专注于你必须做的事情,集中精力完成它。
> 提醒自己,你的任务是做一个好人…
> 然后毫不犹豫地去做,说出你看到的事实。
> 记得带着善良,带着谦卑,不要虚伪。
> 马可·奥勒留

At the same time our goals need to be sufficiently **flexible** to allow for inevitable changes to circumstances. Rigid goals, rigidly upheld, are a recipe for failure, as the world in which we live and operate today changes very rapidly with each new technology.

与此同时,我们的目标需要具有充分的灵活性,以应对不可避免的环境变化。一成不变的目标,教条僵化的经验会导致失败,因为我们生活和面对的世界,随着每一项新技术的产生,都发生着日新月异的变化。

While the overall direction of travel needs continuity, individual goals need to reflect reality as it evolves and changes, with all its complexities.

虽然目标的整体方向需要连贯性,但个别目标也需要反映现实,因为现实是不停演变和变化的,同时具有各种复杂性。

(One of main issues today is that decisions are increasingly rapidly demanded, not least by a restless and insistent public and media, when in fact the issues themselves, for which decisions are required, are often more complex, requiring more time for careful understanding and resolution, before any sensible goals can be set. While 'shooting from the hip' and providing catchy soundbites is quite popular at times, it is a very poor way of establishing meaningful goals, let alone wise decisions.)

(当今社会的一个主要问题是,越来越多的人,尤其是焦躁不安的公众和媒体,被要求以越来越快的速度做出决策。而事实上,需要做出决定的问题,本身往往更加复杂,需要花费更多时间来仔细思索做个抉择,然后才能设定一个合理的目标。虽然有时很时兴"临场发挥"和"动情发言",但对确立有意义的目标,却效果欠佳,更不用说做出明智的决定了。)

None of these matters are easy but then …

做到这些都不容易,但是…

… as Seneca wrote: ***There is not an easy way from the earth to the stars***, and as Louis Pasteur wrote: ***Fortune favours the prepared mind***.

正如塞内卡写道:从地球到星星没有捷径可走;路易斯·巴斯德也曾经说过:幸运之神只会眷顾有准备的人。

The happiness of achieving provides a level of satisfaction that is clearly deeper, longer lasting and more profound than instant gratification.

成就带来的幸福感要远远比即时满足感更深刻、更持久、更强烈。

Its true value, however, resides in what kind of goals we set ourselves, how we have set them and what impact our goals have on our soul and inner harmony and those around us.

然而它的真正价值在于我们给自己设定了什么样的目标，我们是如何设定这些目标的，它们对我们的灵魂和内在和谐以及我们周围的人产生了怎样的影响。

> *As is a tale, so is life:*
> *not how long it is, but how good it is,*
> *is what matters.*
> **Seneca**

> 生命如同一个剧本，重要的不是长度，
> 而是演出的精彩与否。
> 塞内卡

THE THIRD STEP: THE HAPPINESS OF GIVING

第三步：给予带来的幸福感

So far, the achievement of happiness has been predominantly concerned with the self. Instant gratification is about personal happiness based on gratifying one's own wants and mainly about acquiring things, while the happiness of achieving is about succeeding at goals for ourselves.

到目前为止，幸福的实现主要与自我有关。即时满足是基于满足自己需要而获得的个人幸福感，它的重点是获得；而成就带来的幸福感则是成功地实现自己的目标。

To the extent, however, that the goals we set ourselves are for the benefit of others, which they will be if they are about improving other people's lives, or about our own self-improvement in order to be better able to make others happy, then we are into the third stage—the happiness of giving.

然而在某种程度上,如果我们设定的目标是为了他人的利益,是为了改善他人的生活,或者是为了他人更好的幸福而实现自我的完善,那么我们就进入了第三个阶段——给予的快乐。

Research has shown conclusively that once basic material needs are satisfied (food, home, reasonable financial security) there is little if any relationship between the accumulation of wealth and happiness.

研究表明,一旦基本的物质需求得到满足(食物、住房、合理的经济保障),财富积累和幸福之间就几乎没有什么关联了。

Lottery winners have not become significantly happier—often the opposite has been the case—and extremely wealthy people are not significantly happier either. Their wealth often brings in its wake issues of anxiety, health, stress, family discord, social discord and excessive behaviour.

赢得彩票的人并没有变得特别快乐——通常情况恰恰相反——特别富有的人也没有明显变得更快乐。他们的财富往往会带来焦虑不安、健康问题、压力变大、家庭不和、社交不和和其它过度的行为。

There is, however, a strong relationship between giving and happiness.

然而,给予和幸福之间是存在着紧密联系的。

The heart that gives, gathers.
Old English proverb

有舍必有得
—古英文谚语

Studies have shown that people who volunteer and help others enjoy better psychological health. The benefits to mental health are said to be at least as great if not greater than attending religious services or taking up exercise.

研究表明,志愿者和那些愿意帮助他人的人拥有更加健康的心理。帮助他人对保持心理健康的好处相似于(至少不亚于)参加宗教仪式和进行体育锻炼带来的好处。

Studies have also shown that when people whose basic material needs are satisfied were given money, they were happier spending it on others than on themselves. These kinds of financial contribution can be in many forms such as simple charitable giving to setting up charities to look after those in need.

研究同样表明,当人的基本物质需求得到满足时,相比为自己花钱,把钱花在别人身上更让他们幸福。这种财务捐助有很多种方式,如简单的慈善捐款,建立慈善机构来照顾那些需要救助的人。

But giving does not have to entail money at all. Giving of one's talents or one's time, giving advice, support and encouragement, giving as an act of kindness, giving shared laughter and giving love are all acts of giving.

但给予根本并不需要涉及金钱。献出自己的才能或时间,给予别人建议、支持或鼓励,做出善意的举动,分享欢乐和付出爱都是给予的一种。

No one has ever become poor by giving.

没有人会因为给予而变得贫穷。

The happiness derived from these are more than feeling good about oneself but closely related to a **powerful sense of connection and empathy** to others, engendering a more intense feeling of happiness.

由此产生的幸福感不仅仅是自我感觉良好,而是与强烈的人际关系和对他人产生的同理心密切相关,从而带来更加强烈的幸福感。

Before giving, the mind of the giver is happy; while giving, the mind of the giver is made peaceful; and having given, the mind of the giver is uplifted.

在给予之前,他的内心是快乐的;在给予时,他的内心变得平静;给予之后,他的内心得到了升华。

Generosity is about caring for others by being unselfish and thoughtful, not only with our money but also with our time. It is a positive behaviour aimed at enhancing someone else's happiness.

慷慨是无私、体贴地关爱他人,不仅用我们的金钱,还要投入我们的时间。这是一种正向积极的行为,旨在提高他人的幸福感。

The opposite of generosity is 'being mean' which is essentially selfish in that the giver is thinking much more of himself and the negative impact of the gift on him rather than the happiness of the recipient.

慷慨的对立面便是"吝啬",吝啬的本质上是自私的,因为给予者更多的是在考虑自己和即将送出的礼物对自己所产生的负面影响,而非接受者的幸福。

Being generous, altruistic, giving time and energy helping others, volunteering or simply giving of oneself by being kind, compassionate, considerate and thoughtful will enhance well-being and happiness. It will also enhance inner strength.

慷慨大方、无私奉献、付出时间和精力帮助他人，志愿服务或仅仅通过善良、同情和体贴来奉献自己，这都会提高一个人的幸福感，也会增强自己内心的力量。

> *It was our belief that the love of possessions is a weakness to be overcome. Children must learn early the beauty of generosity. They are taught to give what they prize most, that they may taste the happiness of giving …*
> **Charles Alexander Eastman**, also known as **Ohiyesa**

> 我们相信对占有的执着是一种需要克服的弱点。
> 儿童需要及早学会慷慨之美，他们被教导要给予自己最珍视的东西，这样才能尝到给予的快乐…
> 查尔斯·亚历山大·伊斯曼，
> 被人熟知为奥希耶萨(Ohiyesa)

Socrates and Seneca do not directly address the concept of giving. But their philosophy arrives at the same conclusion.

苏格拉底和塞内卡并没有直接提出给予的概念，但他们的哲学思想却得出了同样的结论。

The argument goes like this. If a person examines life carefully, they will learn and attain over time a level of knowledge and gain wisdom. Knowledge and wisdom lead to virtue. Knowledge and wisdom, and hence virtue, must be sought before private interests and are the means by which ethical actions and decisions are made. Virtue is good and good is defined as being beneficial to others.

这个逻辑是这样的。如果一个人仔细地审视人生,随着时间的推移,他就会学到并达到一定的知识水平,获得智慧。知识和智慧通往美德。知识和智慧,以及因此而来的美德必须先于个人利益之前,并且是以合乎道德的方式和行动来完成。美德是善的,而善就是做出对他人有益的事情。

'Beneficial to others' includes any kind of help offered to others including finance, safety, health, well-being, advice, teaching, educating, advising, caring, consoling, influencing in someone's favour and speaking on someone's behalf.

"对他人有益"包括为他人提供任何形式的帮助,包括金钱、安全、健康、福利、建议、教导、教育、咨询、关爱、安慰、对他人产生有利的影响以及为他人发声。

In effect, the virtuous person will naturally want to do what benefits others, which includes all aspects of giving.

实际上,美德会让人自然而然地想做有利于他人的事情,这包括给予的方方面面。

As has already been implied, giving does not have to be material. It takes many forms, but must be done freely and never grudgingly.

正如我们前面所说的,给予不一定是实质性的。它有很多种形式,但必须是不求回报的,绝不是心怀怨念。

For something to count as a benefit, it must be given because that is what the giver wants to do and has chosen to do of their own free will. No other motives must accompany the act of generosity.

做好事,必须是给予者想要这么做,并自愿选择这样做。慷慨大方的行为不应掺杂任何其它动机。

Similarly, it must also be something that is not perceived by the receiver as a burden, an unwanted tie or the creation of a dependence or obligation.

同样,对接受者而言,他所接受的东西不是一种负担,不是一种非必要的联系,不是一种依附关系或义务的开始。

There is an art or style to both giving and receiving. It is something that should be done without fanfare or fuss purely for the joy it brings to both parties. It applies to both the giver and the receiver.

无论是给予还是接受,他们的行为都带有自己的特点或风格。这是一件不应大张旗鼓或大惊小怪的事情,它纯粹是为了给双方带来快乐。这既适用于给予者,也适用于接受者。

It is not uncommon for people who are givers to find it hard to be receivers. They are happy to give compliments, advice, help and support but find it difficult to receive or to be as gracious when receiving.

有时,给予者会难以接受别人的给予。他们乐意给出自己的赞美、建议、帮助和支持,而一旦自己成为被给予的对象时,他们就会表现出一定的抗拒。

It is as if they feel they are not worthy of this treatment, partly out of a sense of modesty, partly because they feel they have somehow not deserved the praise or support and partly because they feel they should not need praise or help.

他们感觉自己不值得被这样对待,一部分是因为自谦,一部分是因为觉得自己不配得到或不需要他人的赞扬或帮助。

Giving and taking should be seen as part of the same process, and the same respect needs to be shown by both parties.

给予和接受应被视为同一进程的两部分,双方都应表现出同样的尊重。

To brush off the compliment is to dishonour, however unwittingly, the giver and make them feel confused, and perhaps unhappy.

对别人的赞美置之不理,是对给予者的不尊重,不管这种不尊重是有意为之还是无心之举,都会让给予者感到困惑,甚至感到沮丧。

A simple, honest 'thank you' will often suffice, but it is surprising how often such an effective acknowledgement is forgotten.

通常情况下,一句简单真诚的"谢谢"就已足够,但令人诧异的是,这样如此有效的致谢方法却常常被忽略。

Every relationship is one of give and take. Giving engenders receiving and receiving engenders giving. ... In reality ... giving and receiving are different aspects of the flow of energy in the universe. ... Practicing the Law of Giving is actually very simple: if you want joy, give joy to others; if you want love, learn to give love; if you want attention and appreciation, learn to give attention and appreciation ...
Deepak Chopra

每一种关系都包含着给予和获得。付出产生接受,接受换来给予。...在现实生活中,给予和接受是宇宙能量流动的不同方面。...实践给予的法则其实很简单,
如果你想要快乐,就先给别人带来快乐;
如果你想得到爱,就先学会爱别人;如果你想得到关注和赞美,就先给予别人关注和赞美...

狄巴克·乔布拉

Giving and receiving need to be in balance.

给予和接受之间需要保持一定的平衡。

If the receiver is unable to receive or to respond with gratitude or happiness but rather feels guilty or powerless, then balance cannot be achieved and continuing to give only makes the situation worse.

如果接受者无法接受,或无法用幸福和感激来回应,反而对此感到内疚或无能为力,那么给予和接受之间就无法保持平衡,继续给予只会让情况变得更糟糕。

Under such circumstances, giving alone will lead to unhappiness. Receiving, just as giving, needs to be learned. It requires dignity and grace as it is our response to what others are giving of themselves to us.

在这种情况下,一味地付出只会导致不幸的发生。接受和给予一样都需要学习,接受需要尊严和优雅,这是我们对别人给予的回应。

What does one person give to another?
He gives of himself, of the most precious he has,
he gives of his life. This does not necessarily mean
that he sacrifices his life for the other — but that he
gives him of that which is alive in him; he gives him
of his joy, of his interest, of his understanding, of
his knowledge, of his humour, of his sadness —
of all expressions and manifestations of that which
is alive in him. In thus giving of his life, he enriches
the other person, he enhances the other's sense of
aliveness by enhancing his own sense of aliveness.
He does not give in order to receive; giving is in itself
exquisite joy. But in giving he cannot help bringing
something to life in the other person, and this which
is brought to life reflects back to him; in truly giving,
he cannot help receiving that which is given back
to him. Giving implies to make the other person a
giver also and they both share in the joy of what they
have brought to life. In the act of giving something is
born, and both persons involved are grateful
for the life that is born for both of them.
Erich Fromm

一个人能给予另外一个人什么？他可以献出自己，献出他所拥有的最宝贵的东西，献出他的人生。这并不一定意味着他为别人牺牲了自己的生命-而是他把自己的内在给了别人；他把他的快乐、他的乐趣、他的理解、他的知识、他的幽默、他的悲伤-所有的情感和表达都是他的内在。在这样的给予中，他丰富了他人的生活，通过提升自己的活力来提升他人的活力。他的给予并不是为了得到,给予本身就是一种美妙的快乐。但是在给予的过程中,他会在不知情的情况下复苏接受者身上的某种特质,而这种复苏的特质也会反映在他身上;在真正的给予中,他会不由自主的的得到接受者的赠予。给予也意味着让双方都成为给予者,彼此分享给予给生活带来的快乐。在给予的过程中,新事物就这样诞生了,给予者和接受者双方都对此充满感激。
艾瑞克·弗洛姆

The happiness of giving is a universal happiness in that it transcends all cultures and creeds and is a fundamental step towards universal harmony.

给予所带来的快乐是全人类共同的幸福感,这种幸福感超越了所有的文化和信仰,是走向普世和谐的重要步骤。

Gentleness, self-sacrifice and generosity are the exclusive possession of no one race or religion.
Mahatma Gandhi

仁慈、自我牺牲和慷慨不是一个种族或宗教独有的特质。
圣雄甘地

THE FOURTH STEP: THE HAPPINESS OF RELATIONSHIPS

第四步:人际关系带来的幸福感

The happiness of relationships is all about giving and receiving, with the added notion of deep personal, emotional, physical and spiritual love for others.

人际关系的幸福在于给予和接受,伴随着对他人个体的深刻的情感、身体及精神层次的热爱。

In this respect, it builds on the happiness of giving and adds an extra dimension. Strong relationships are joyful precisely because they are what is best in human nature, and human being are social beings who depend and thrive on positive social interactions. The closer and genuinely more heartfelt these interactions, the deeper the connection and the greater the level of happiness.

从这一方面来说,它建立在给予的快乐之上,并增加了一个额外的维度。牢固的人际关系是令人愉悦的,因为它是人性中最美好的东西,而人类是依靠积极的社交互动不断繁衍成长的社会群体。这些互动越紧密、越真诚、越交心,彼此之间的联系就越深,幸福的程度也就越高。

Such connections are very special and quite rare. They take time and patience to develop and require understanding, empathy, common values and an intimately shared sense of what matters in life and in the world.

这种联系是非常特殊和罕见的,它需要花费时间和耐心来维系,需要对彼此的理解、共情、共同的价值观以及对生活和世界中的重要事物有着共同的认识。

Above all they require a deep desire to care, to cherish the other person unconditionally and to uplift them whenever possible.

最重要的是,这种联系的建立需要发自内心的无条件的关爱、珍惜,并在对方需要鼓励的时候给予他们力量。

To achieve this level of connection in any relationship is difficult, and there are many potential obstacles.

要想在任何一段关系中达到如此紧密的程度是非常困难的,并且还存在着许多潜在的障碍。

These need to be understood in order to be overcome.

要克服这些困难,就要先对困难进行一番了解。

In the paragraphs below, we examine a number of key issues.

在接下来的各段落中,我们会分析一些关键性问题。

Relationships need symmetry

人际关系需要对称性

Relationships need to be in balance and harmonious if they are to succeed.

平衡与和谐的关系才是成功的关系。

A relationship is 'symmetrical' when each is giving and taking in equal measure and the relationship is based on sound *shared* values, then it has the potential to lead to the wonderful happiness that comes when one soul discovers and appreciates another.

每一个人都平等地给予和接受,并且将关系建立在合理的共同价值观基础上,这就是"对称"的关系。当一个灵魂最终发现并欣赏另一个灵魂时,这种关系就有可能会给双方带来美妙的幸福感。

Friendship arises out of mere companionship when two or more companions discover that they have in common some insight or interest or even taste which the others do not share and which, till that moment, each believed to be his unique treasure (or burden). The typical expression of opening friendship would be something like, "what? You too? I thought I was the only one."
CS Lewis

两个或两个以上的同伴发现他们拥有共同的见解、兴趣甚至与他人截然不同的品味时,友谊就此产生了。直到那一刻,每个人都以为这些见解、兴趣和品位是自己所独有的特质(或负担),直到在友谊开诚布公的那一刻,大家的反应才是"原来你和我是一样的想法。"
CS 路易斯

A symmetrical relationship is one of mutual trust, peace, calm, respect, honour, freedom and love, where each feels the same for the other and contributes wholeheartedly to the relationship.

对称关系是一种相互信任、和谐、平静、敬重、尊敬、自由和关爱的关系，双方都对彼此有同样的感觉，并全心全意地为这段关系付出。

Nothing is unsaid. There are no elephants in the room that no one wants to address. It is OK to raise anything since the approach to any issue is to find a sensible solution together—rather than find fault or to judge.

没有避而不谈的难言之隐。在这段关系中，提出任何问题都是可以的，因为对双方来说，共同努力找到一个明智的解决方案要比吹毛求疵或相互指责重要得多。

Differences of views and opinions are aired openly and easily with the objective of finding common, acceptable solutions or just agreeing to disagree, which is fine too. There is no sense of 'winning' or 'losing' since both gain. Even heated arguments result in hugs and laughter.

公开地向对方表达出不同的意见和观点是为了找到共同的、可接受的解决方案，或者最后双方还是各执己见，这也没什么不对。因为在这个沟通的过程中，没有什么"胜利"或"失败"之分，这是一个双赢的局面。即使是激烈的争论最后也会在拥抱和笑声中得到化解。

Good relationships are not about being in agreement about everything. They are about acceptance, tolerance, compassion, respect, reverence and caring.

良好的人际关系并不是说双方能够在所有的事情上都达成一致,而是关乎相互接受、宽容、同情、尊重、敬畏和关心。

Relationships are based on four principles: respect, understanding, acceptance and appreciation.
Mahatma Gandhi

人际关系的基础是建立在四个原则之上的:尊重、理解、接受和感激。
圣雄甘地

Symmetrical relationships happen with partners, friends, siblings and family, or within associations, groups and teams and are encompassed within the five words for love that the Ancient Greeks used, especially *philia*.

伴侣、朋友、兄弟姐妹和家人之间通常是对称关系,亦或者在团队、协会、组织中,这种情感都包含在古希腊人所总结的五种爱里,尤其是philia这个词。

On the other hand, some relationships are or can become 'asymmetrical', that is to say one partner or friend is giving much more, or **feels or believes** they are giving much more to the relationship than the other.

另一方面,有些关系是"不对称的",或者会向这个方向演变,因为其中的一方或朋友在这段关系中付出了更多,或者说他们感觉或相信自己是付出比较多的那个人。

This can also occur when the needs of one (whether for reassurance or control) are very different or more intense than the needs of the other.

当一方的需求(无论是为了得到肯定还是控制权)与另一方完全不同,或者他拥有比对方更加强烈的需求,"不对称"关系就此产生了。

Or when the partners, not sharing the same values or with different approaches to life or to people, begin to feel they are not on the same wavelength and talk at cross purposes.

又或者当两个人的价值观不同,面对生活和对待他人的态度也不同时,他们开始意识到自己和对方的想法并不一致,并都错误的理解了对方的意思。

Asymmetry also arises when the quality of listening skill is sadly lacking or when there is an absence of true caring and compassion.

当其中一方不善于倾听或对对方缺乏真正的关心和同情时,也会产生不对称的关系。

Or when there is a high degree of judgment, based, as it must inevitably be, on the limitations of our own attitudes, beliefs and expectations.

不可避免的是,与此相对应的较高的评判标准是受我们自己的态度、信仰和期望值所局限的。

All such relationships have a high risk of becoming unhappy—toxic even—very quickly. And toxicity brings unhappiness and distress.

这样的关系存在变得让人不再愉悦的高风险—甚至可能很快变得有毒。而有毒的关系只会给人带来不幸和痛苦。

The causes of such problems need to be examined carefully and resolved, before the relationship becomes irretrievably damaged.

在关系受到不可挽回的伤害之前,我们需要仔细检查出现问题的原因,并对其加以解决。

Why and how does this happen? What are the circumstances that create the imbalance? Why is this more likely between some individuals than others?

为什么会这样,怎么会这样?造成关系不对称的原因是什么?为什么这种情况会更容易发生在某些人身上?

There are multiple reasons and we will explore several of them in order to provide guidance and advice on how to address each issue, learn important new skills and thus substantially increase the chances of a successful and happy outcome.

产生的原因有很多,我们将探讨其中的几个以便为解决每个问题提供指导和建议,并学一些重要的技能,从而大大增加成功和获得愉快结果的机会。

The first thing to examine is what happens in the mind when individuals first meet. We can then discover why people react the way they do based on their own personality preferences, what to do to manage this process and how to unblock potential problems.

首先要分析的是在人们在初次会面时,他们给彼此留下了什么印象。通过这个分析我们就能发现,个性偏好怎么影响到他们的行为和反应,以及如何处理好这个过程并消除可能的潜在问题。

This will provide the key to establishing successful relationships with anyone.

这是和他人建立成功关系的关键。

Establishing rapport

建立融洽友好的往来

When strangers meet each other for the first time, especially in unfamiliar locations or situations, there is a very rapid first reaction from a most primitive part of the brain, the amygdala, which is responsible for heightening our awareness of danger and perception of fear, anger, sadness and aggression, preparing the body to fight or flee.

彼此陌生的人第一次见面时,尤其是在一个极其陌生的地点或环境下见面,作为大脑中最原始的一部分——杏仁核,会产生非常迅速的第一反应,它负责提高我们对危险的意识,以及对恐惧、愤怒、悲伤和挑衅的感知,并为可能发生的身体对抗或逃跑做好准备。

This is a natural defence mechanism, which was most valuable at a time when life was hazardous and split-second decisions were required for survival. Decisions had to be made quickly. Friend or foe? Do I need to run away fast, or get ready to fight?

这是一种天生的防御机制,当我们面对危险命悬一线,需要在零秒的内做出决定时,它发挥的作用就尤为重要。对方是敌是友?我需要快速逃跑还是准备战斗?

In most of the situations we experience today, which are generally much less threatening, these reactions, whilst still present, are much more subdued.

在我们今天所经历的大多数情况下,事情并没有那么强烈的威胁性,但这种防御机制依然存在,只不过要温和得多。

They can express themselves, though, in such forms as mild aggression, excessive or overly hard handshaking, looking away, and sullenness or even (especially in the case of angst-ridden teenagers) a refusal to say hello altogether.

这种防御机制依然有办法表达自己,如轻微的攻击性、过度用力的握手、转移视线、闷闷不乐,甚至(尤其常见于情绪处于焦躁不安的青少年)完全拒绝与人交流。

Once these preliminaries are over, the subconscious mind takes over and decides what attitude to take to the stranger. How does it do this?

一旦这些前期准备工作完成,潜意识就会占据主导地位,它将决定以什么样的态度面对陌生人。潜意识是如何做到这些的呢?

The subconscious mind has stored the detail of all previous encounters and selects the ones that most fit the current situation. It has stored how people looked, dressed, behaved and acted, how loud or quiet they were, how fascinating or boring they appeared to be and makes a judgment based on this mass of historical data, however inaccurate it may be.

潜意识保存了之前所有遇到的细节,并对最适合当前情况的细节加以选择。它保存了人们的外貌、衣着、行为举止、声音大小和安静程度,以及他们看上去是魅力四射还是无聊透顶,并对这些大量的并不完全准确的数据进行分析判断。

It uses this information primarily to protect its host. The subconscious mind is in fact **looking for itself**. It is looking for **someone like me**, its **mirror image**, because someone like me is likely to be the best and safest option.

它利用这些信息保护我们。实际上,潜意识是在寻找它自己,是在寻找与我们相似的人,在寻找我们的镜像,因为与我们相似的人才有可能是最好最安全的选择。

When strangers assemble for the first time, it can be observed how, fairly rapidly, they form into groups.

陌生人第一次聚集在一起时,我们可以观察到人群是如何群分形成小组的。

These groups will appear, at least on the surface, to be very homogeneous and the homogeneity will be in terms of participants' age, gender, appearance, clothing, hairstyle, facial expression and/or social background.

这些小群体的成员,至少从表面来看,都具有一定的共同点,比如:年龄、性别、衣着、发型、面部表情及社会背景方面。

The whole process is entirely subconscious. The subconscious mind of each participant is making judgments on 'who is most like me' and naturally gravitating towards them.

整个过程完全是被潜意识所主导。每个成员的潜意识都在对"和我最像"做出判断,并自然而然地向他们靠拢。

As the participants start to know and understand each other better, the groupings will change quite naturally as the subconscious mind makes adjustments based on new data and updated assessments on who is 'most like me'.

随着相互认识和了解的逐渐加深,潜意识会根据最新的数据对"和我最像"的人进行评估和调整,分组也就成了水到渠成的事情。

But what does 'most like me' mean? What are the elements that the subconscious mind is looking for as it makes its assessments?

但"和我最像"到底意味着什么？潜意识进行评估的根据又是什么？

This needs careful examination in order to be able to manage and develop meaningful, satisfying and beneficial relationships **even when two people are not like each other**.

即使两个人毫无共同之处，潜意识也会对其进行仔细地研究和检查，从而发展出一段有意义的、令人愉悦的，同时，对双方都有益的关系。

Establishing just such relationships is important, valuable and enriching precisely because it enables a wider perspective to be taken, new knowledge and understanding to be gleaned and wisdom to be acquired from sources not usually tapped. Why deprive yourself of such an opportunity just because someone appears to be different?

建立起这样的关系是一个非常重要并能够充实自己的机会，因为它能够开拓我们的视野，使我们学习到新的知识和领悟，并能够从不常用的渠道中汲取智慧。为什么仅仅因为他看起来与众不同就剥夺了这样的机会呢？

Numerous psychographic studies have been conducted on this topic over many years, but there is much still to discover and learn.

多年来，人们对这一课题进行了大量的心理研究，但还有很多值得深入挖掘和研究的地方。

Here is one analysis of the six areas that have the most significant impact on relationships and on understanding what 'most like me' means.

以下是对六个方面的分析，这六个方面对人际关系和对"和我最像"的含义有着重大影响。

The six areas are: energy and drive; the way information is viewed and assimilated; the way decisions are taken; lifestyle management; empathy, warmth and sincerity; and a sense of humour.

这六个方面包括：精力和动力、对信息的接收和理解、决策方式、生活态度的管理、同理心、热情和真诚，以及幽默感。

Energy and drive

精力与动力

People's energy and drive can be anywhere on a line between high and low.

人类的精力和能量体现在不同的领域,具体的表现也有高有低。

High energy, high drive people, who are often referred to as 'extroverts, will naturally gravitate to likeminded souls and will be happy talking and exchanging views at length and sometimes quite noisily over long periods of time.

精力充沛、活力四射的人通常被称为"外向者",他们会很自然地被志趣相投的人所吸引,并乐于长篇大论地谈论和交换彼此的意见,有时甚至会过于喧哗。

They **gain more energy** from these exchanges and will seem to have a substantial capacity for socializing. They are happy to get on their soap box and may be difficult to stop. Their energy comes from and is increased by the exchanges they have with other people.

通过这些交流,他们获得了更多的能量,看起来好像也拥有了更强大的社交能力。他们非常乐意发表自己的意见,并且很难停下来。他们的精力来源于与他人的交流,在交流的过程中,他们的精力也变得越发充沛。

On the other hand, low energy, low drive people, often referred to as 'introverts', derive their energy from 'me time', when they can relax and recover on their own, because they become exhausted rather than exhilarated by exchanges with other people.

与此相反的是,精力低下、缺乏动力的人通常被称为"内向者",他们的能量来自于"自我时间",一个人独处的时候,他们可以放松并做回自己,而和其他人的交流只会让他们感到疲惫不堪。

They can perform perfectly well during such interactions, but they will need to recharge their energy batteries sooner and more frequently. They need their **quiet time**.

在和其他人的交流过程中,他们也可以表现得很好,但他们需要及时、频繁地为自己的能量电池充电,需要自我独处的安静时间。

These two types are very different and have very **different needs**.

这两种人的性格大相径庭,他们的需求也各不相同。

When they come together, the differences they have on this dimension creates an obvious potential for discord. While one is getting more and more animated, the other is getting more and more tired, so that the possibility of misunderstanding becomes greater: one risks been seen as brash and loud, the other as dull and boring.

当这两种人走到一起时,他们在这个层面上的差异就会造成明显的不和谐。一个人变得越来越活跃时,另一个人却觉得越发疲惫,因此而产生误解的可能性也就越来越大,即一方被认为是鲁莽喧闹,另一方被认为是无聊透顶。

With skillful management, however, these differences can be understood and overcome in the longer term.

然而,经过有技巧的沟通管理,这些分歧可以在较长时间内得到理解和克服。

To start with, the differences need to be acknowledged and respected, with a full exposure of why and how these differences are occurring. This is followed either by an open discussion on what actions to take to mitigate the problem or, with experience, a personal reflection on what is happening and appropriate adjustment made to **one's own behaviour**.

首先,需要理解和尊重彼此之间的差异,并充分明白导致分歧产生的原因和方式。然后,要么大家开诚布公的讨论缓和问题的办法,要么根据经验对存在的问题进行反思,并对自己的行为做出适当的调整。

If we want to change how the exchange goes and the perception one is creating, the change has to be from the inside of oneself first. Any attempt to change anyone else is wrong and arrogant and will fail.

如果我们想要改变交流的方式和对事物的见解,首先要从改变自己的内心开始。任何试图改变他人的尝试都是错误且傲慢的,并最终会失败。

Only then can solutions be found to accommodate the differences and turn a potentially difficult relationship into a positive one.

只有这样才能找到解决方法,容纳分歧的存在,从而将一种潜在的困难重重的关系转变为积极向上的关系。

Consider this case. A married couple were both lecturers and professors in the same subject on the same, well-attended and acclaimed management courses. Both were highly regarded by the faculty and by students.

试想一下这个案例。有这样一对已婚夫妇,他们同时在同一门课程担任讲师和教授,这是一门学习人数很多、广受好评的课程。这对夫妇的教学水平都得到了同事和学生的高度认可。

The wife was high energy, high drive, and extroverted, the husband low energy, low drive and more introverted. When they conducted their course, they would perform very professionally and achieved consistently high rates for their lectures and the management of their courses.

妻子是个精力充沛、活力四射、性格外向的人,而丈夫是个精力低下、沉默寡言、性格内向的人。在教授课程时,他们都表现得非常专业,并在讲座和课程管理方面都取得了傲人的成绩。

The issues, however, would surface in the post-lecture period.

然而,问题出现在课后时间。

The high energy, high drive lecturer was happy to mingle with the students till late in the evening and considered it part of her role, while the low energy, low drive lecturer needed his quiet time and would slip away early to recuperate.

精力充沛、活力四射的妻子喜欢和学生们打成一片,一直陪伴他们至深夜,认为这是她作为讲师的职责之一。

而精力低下、沉默寡言的丈夫则需要独处的安静时光,他会早早溜走进行自我修复。

This was starting to create serious problems in their relationship.

这开始给他们的关系带来严重的问题。

The high energy, high drive lecturer felt that she was shouldering the greater part of the workload and was contributing much more to supporting the students after work.

精力充沛、活力四射的讲师认为自己承担了大部分的工作量,在课余时间里为学生们付出了更多的心血。

The low energy, low drive lecturer felt unappreciated for his highly competent lecturing skills, careful reflections on the course content and ongoing adjustments to it. He also felt somewhat demotivated and tired.

精力低下、沉默寡言的讲师则感觉自己高超的教学技巧、对课程内容的仔细研究和不断调整并没有得到赏识,他也感到有些沮丧和厌倦。

The relationship was becoming asymmetrical.

这段关系开始变得不对称了。

It was at this point that they sought help.

针对这一点,他们开始寻求帮助。

This was the solution:

解决方案如下:

1. To ensure that both parties understood fully what the differences in energy levels were and how each had differing needs for recuperation. It was not that the low energy lecturer was unable to mingle or that he did not wish to do so, it was simply that he needed to create quiet time during which he could recharge his batteries, if he was to undertake this task with the enthusiasm it warranted.

   Similarly, the high energy lecturer needed to understand that her highly intense post lecture activities were not necessarily always welcome by the students, who also had their differing energy needs, as well as the requirement to study. She also needed to appreciate the important work being done by her husband on the course content in between sessions and that reflecting on the course content and making adjustments based on these reflections was a shared responsibility.

1. 确保双方充分理解精力水平的差异,以及各自对自我修复方式的不同需求。这并不意味着性格内向的讲师不能或不希望与人交流,而是他需要为自己营造一个安静的时间,在此期间,他可以为自己充电,从而以应有的热情来完成任务。

   同样,精力充沛的讲师需要明白,她所安排的高度紧张的课后活动不一定是学生所需要的,他们自己也有不同的精力需求和学习欲望。同时,她还要欣赏丈夫在上课期间对课程内容做出的重要工作,并且认识到根据学生们的反应对课程内容进行仔细研究和调整是他们共同的责任。

2. To adjust the work and lecture schedule (and build in reflection time) to create space for recuperation and thus enable the low energy, low drive lecturer to participate in post-lecture activities.

   They also agreed that, after a period of post-lecture activity, they would both leave at the same time, showing alignment and harmony on the part of the lecturers and allowing time for the students to complete their assignments.

2. 调整工作和讲课时间(设立课程内思考的时间)从而为自我修复创造空间,使精力低下、沉默寡言的讲师参与到课余活动中。

   他们还一致同意在经过一段时间的课余活动

后,他们将会同时离开,以显示讲师们之间的协调性,并给学生留出时间完成作业。

The solution was therefore based on an open discussion of what was happening in the mind of the two lecturers, why they felt the way they did, a proper understanding of the differences that existed and then a creative and sympathetic give-and-take approach to its resolution.

因此,解决方法是两个讲师开诚布公地谈论各自的想法,沟通产生这种感觉的原因,正确理解彼此间的差异,然后秉着创意和相互体谅的心,商量着找到解决问题。

The way information is viewed and assimilated

对信息的接收和理解

People absorb information and manage it in very different ways.

每个人接受和处理信息的方式各不相同。

In order to make sense of the information received, some will look for big pictures, exciting patterns and connections while others will look for detail and logical understanding.

为了理解所接收到的信息，有的人会着眼全局，寻找独特的模式和关联，有的人则会注重细节和逻辑思维。

The first group will be more interested in creative aspects while the other will be more interested in analytical aspects.

第一种人对创造性事物更感兴趣，另外一种人则对分析事物更为敏感。

The creative group will use more of the right side of the brain to stimulate their imagination, developing ideas, concepts and images of what the possibilities might be. They will create opportunities from the information received and enjoy the visions they have created—even if they are sometimes rather optimistic!

创意思维占主导的人会更多地使用他们的右脑来刺激想象力，产生各种各样的想法、概念和可能性的图像。他们会从接收到的信息中创造机会，并沉浸在他们所创造的愿景中——即使有时候他们会表现得过于乐观。

The analytical group, unimpressed by the flights of fancy and woolly 'blue sky thinking' of the creative group, will take a calm, serious, sceptical approach and ensure in their own minds that the information they have received adds up, makes sense and is logically correct. Until they reach that point, they will feel distinctly uncomfortable. The certainty they need is missing.

偏向分析思维的人不会被那些异想天开的,甚至"天马行空"的想法所打动,他们会采取冷静、严肃、怀疑的态度,并确保自己收到的信息是合情合理、逻辑分明的。在信息没有得到确认之前,他们会感到极度的不舒服,因为他们对此没有把握。

Many a project or plan has failed miserably because the creative group's enthusiasm was not tempered by the analytical group's wise common sense. And the schemes that they dreamt up were sometimes much more expensive, a source of friction and disharmony and ultimately unworkable.

很多项目和计划惨遭失败,是因为创意思维没有与逻辑思维相调和。创意性头脑中想出的方案实施起来的要求更高,也是产生摩擦和分歧的根源,最终使方案无法实施。

There **was** someone in the group, which consisted mainly of creative types, with an appropriately analytical mind, who could have helped. Carried by their enthusiastic reverie, none of the 'creatives' thought to ask them their opinion. They would most likely have been considered spoilsports and boring and ignored anyway.

通向幸福的阶梯

一个团队中,有些被归类在了创造力思维群体中的人,是具有足够的分析能力的,他们原本可以更好地帮助一些创意性项目落地。然而在狂热遐想的簇拥下,没有一个"创意者"想要征求他们的意见。又或者,他们要是对可行性提出质疑的话,很可能被其他成群员认为败兴、无趣,最终被无视。

Similarly, many brilliant projects have been abandoned because the analytical types, who represented the majority, could not get 'the numbers to add up' and never gained the certainty they craved. Had they asked the creative type whether some changes could be made to improve the financials and reduce the uncertainty and risk, they could have transformed the project into a significant success. But they didn't trust the creative person sufficiently to ask.

同样,很多优秀的项目,却因为决策群体中占大多数的分析思维认为"不够务实",也因为无法得到他们渴望的确定性而搁置。如果这些分析能力至上的人能向拥有创造性思维的人求助,找到方法改善财务状况,减少不确定性和风险,就可以把这个项目转变为巨大的成功。但是因为他们对拥有创造性思维的人缺乏信任,所以没有提出这样的要求。

As individuals, couples or groups we need both types of thinking in our lives.

不论是个人、伴侣还是团队，我们的生活中都需要这两种思维的人存在。

We need to have access to creativity and imaginative thinking as well as an understanding of detail and workability. One without the other is always going to run the risk of being sub-optimal.

我们即需要拥有创造力和想象力，也不能缺乏对细节和可操作性的理解。缺乏其中任何一个，都不是我们的最佳选择。

Understanding this fact and actively seeking both is essential to mental development and growth as well as excellent relationships.

充分理解这一点并积极寻求这两者的同意，对个人的心智发展和成长，以及建立良好的人际关系都是至关重要的。

While the differences in the way information is processed will tend to divide the two types, seeking out those with different approaches is extremely important, to avoid costly mistakes and also to stimulate and stretch the mind, find innovative solutions and learn.

因为接收处理信息的方式不同，才出现了以创新思维为主和以分析思维为主的两种人。但采用不同的方法处理自己接收到的信息是极其重要的，以避免代价高昂的重大错误。这样做同时也能刺激和拓展我们的思维，找出创新型的解决方法、学到新的知识。

The way decisions are taken

决策的制定方式

The continuum here is between decision-making based predominantly on emotions and decision-making based on results.

决策方式的差异主要在于基于情感的决策和基于结果的决策。

The group who are emotion based will take decisions when they **feel comfortable** with it. If others are involved in the decision, they will delay until such time as they **feel that everybody is comfortable**.

以感情为决策基础的人会在他们感到舒服的时候做出决定。如果整个决策过程还涉及到其他人，他们会不断拖延，直到他们感觉每个人都感到舒服的时候再做出决定。

Until then, they will question and probe, suggest alternatives, try different approaches, even abandon the decision altogether or at the very least delay it. Time is less important than alignment.

否则,他们会不断地进行质疑和调查、提出替代方案、尝试不同的方法,甚至完全放弃做决定,至少推迟做决定的时间。与时间相比,意见统一更为重要。

A potential pitfall at this stage is that 'analysis paralysis' occurs. No decision is taken because there never is enough information with which to be comfortable enough to take one. And there never will be! Complete certainty does not exist and there is always risk in any decision.

这一阶段存在的潜在陷阱是"分析瘫痪"(即过度分析带来的优柔寡断)。不能做出决策是因为决策者总是觉得没有收集到足够的信息,没有十足的把握可以做出正确的决定。永远都不会有的!完全的确定性是不存在的,任何决策都存在一定的风险。

What is often forgotten, however, is that sometimes the greatest risk lies in doing nothing, postponing, asking for more studies, doing more research, anything to avoid making a decision. This then becomes a fear of getting it wrong and ultimately being blamed or blaming oneself (a vestige of past parental expectations).

然而常常被人忽视的是,有时最大的风险却是坐以待毙、一推再推、总是要做更多的研究和调查或回避任何需要做出决定的事情。演变成了一种恐惧,惧怕犯

错，害怕最终自己受到指责或感到自责。(这是过去父母对自己期望所留下的痕迹)

No decisions can be based on perfect information or perfect alignment or hundred percent certainty. Life is not like that. Allowing this to become a wonderful excuse for indecision and to waste time on seeking alignment with others or **alignment with one's own mind** is a recipe for anxiety and unhappiness. It reduces one's inner strength.

没有任何决策是基于完美无误的信息或完美精确的统一意见，或者百分之百的确定性而做出。人生不是这样的。这种要求会成为优柔寡断的绝佳借口，浪费时间去寻求与他人的一致或追寻符合自己预期的设想都会导致焦虑和痛苦，会削弱一个人的内在力量。

Another risk of this group is that the search for alignment leads to a sub-standard result, especially if the people who are part of the process are all predominantly emotion-driven decision takers. They may opt for the solution that they can all feel comfortable with but which is itself the worst one and a poor compromise. *They have preferred alignment to action.*

感情用事的人所面对的另一个风险是一味地寻求意见的统一，从而产生不符合标准的结果，尤其是当参与决策过程的人都是容易被情绪主导的决策者时。他们会选择一个所有人都感到满意的方案,但这本身就是一个糟糕的方案,而且是一个极其糟糕的折中方案。相比做出行动,意见的统一对他们来说更为重要。

The group who have preference to action, on the other hand, will take decisions based on **achieving a result**, preferably in the most efficient and timely manner possible. The problem is that, in their mind, if others don't like it, it's just too bad! This is a recipe for resentment and rejection.

另一方面,行动派的人则依据结果为导向做出决策,并尽可能以最有效、最迅速的方式做出决策。问题是,对他们而言,如果别人不欣赏他们的决定,就太可惜了!而且还会引起怨恨和排斥。

To this group, alignment is less important than efficiency and time management. *Urgency requires quick decisions. Taking time to get everyone on board is a luxury that they believe doesn't exist.*

对于这类人来说,效率和时限要比一致性更为重要。紧急情况需要快速做出决策。花费时间调动所有人对他们来说是一种不存在的奢侈。

The obvious risk here is that decisions are made quickly and arbitrarily without considering their full effect, especially on other people. No time is devoted to ensuring there is a 'buy-in' either in one's own mind or by colleagues. We are all human beings who act based on how we feel rather than what we may logically believe.

这里显而易见的风险是决策的做出是迅速且武断的，决策者并没有考虑到它所带来的全部影响，特别是对他人的影响。没有花时间确保得到自己内心或同事的"认同"。我们人类的行动都是根据自己的感觉，而非逻辑或信仰。

***When dealing with people remember
you are not dealing with creatures of logic,
but creatures of emotion.***

在与人交往的过程中，
记住你不是在与逻辑主导性生物进行沟通，
人都是情感主导性的。

Taking decisions that affect others without due consideration for their feelings or the impact this will have on them is a recipe for discord and disharmony.

作出影响他人的决定，而不适当考虑他们的感受或对他们产生的影响，是导致不和谐和分歧的根源。

If people feel ignored or bullied, they will be hurt and resentful and, as in physics, there will be an equal and opposite reaction. This resentment has been known to lead to actions to sabotage the plan.

人一旦觉得自己受到了忽视或者被欺负了,就会感到受伤,产生怨恨。就像在物理学中,每一个作用力都存在着一个与其大小相同、方向相反的反作用力,这种怨恨也会转化成为破坏决策的行动力。

Obviously this can be the cause of considerable stress when the two extremes meet.

显然,当这两个思想极端的群体相遇时,巨大的压力就产生了。

One wants to be sure all options have been examined and everyone is happy with the decision, while the other simply wants to get it done.

一部分人想要确保所有的决定都经过了仔细的考察,并且得到了每个人的赞同,而另一部分人只是想尽快把事情完成。

Here again, there are no right or wrongs. It all depends on the circumstances.

这其实没有什么对错之分,都要视情况而定。

If alignment is important—for example, when several people are involved or when the individual is unsure on which course to take and needs to consult widely before making a decision—then basing the decision on the emotions being satisfied is perfectly sensible.

在一致性很重要的情况下,比如说:当决策的制定涉及到许多人;或者个人不确定要选择哪种方式,需要广泛征求大家的意见时;那么把决定建立在满足情感的基础上是完全明智的。

Similarly, when time is short and decisions are needed, then achieving a decision efficiently and quickly is also perfectly sensible and pragmatic. You don't need to get everybody aligned if the house is on fire!

同样,在时间紧急的情况下,快速高效地做出决定也是非常明智和实际的。就像房子失火了,你不需要得到每个人的同意才去救火。

Dealing with this is, once again, based on understanding the situation realistically first.

需要再次强调的是,处理这种问题首先要正确地理解当前的形势。

Is alignment of all the participants really that critical? Will the decision-makers or participants be happy with a majority point of view? Is it really necessary to take that decision right now rather than 'sleep on it'? Would a few more searches, or enquiries or another study not be worth waiting for?

所有参与者的一致性真的那么重要吗？决策者和参与者会乐意接受多数人的观点吗？真的有必要现在就做决定，而不是经过深思熟虑、仔细考量吗？多做一些研究和调查真的没有必要吗？

Understanding the situation and the underlying needs and wants of each person involved and the extent to which they can contribute to the decision is also important. Do they have knowledge vital to the decision or is their need really to be acknowledged or just to be asked?

了解情况，理解每个参与者的根本需求和愿望，以及他们对决策的贡献程度也很重要。他们是否拥有做决策所必须的关键知识，或者他们的需求是否真的一定要得到满足，还是只需要对决策有简单的知情权就好。

Knowing and reflecting on these underlying issues will often enable a wiser decision to be taken, perhaps even quicker and without running roughshod over the emotions of the participants.

相比只是粗暴忽略参与者的情绪，了解并考虑这些根本性的问题往往会使人们做出更快、更明智的决定

Lifestyle management

生活态度的管理

Some people are naturally more relaxed about their lives, while others have higher stress levels. Some are happy to 'go with the flow' while others have a greater need to plan and organize. Differences in life management can be the source of significant anxiety and disharmony.

有些人天生就是乐天派,有些人则是焦虑派。有些人乐于"一切顺其自然",有些人则更注重井井有条的秩序。生活习惯上的差异可能是造成严重焦虑和极度不和谐的根源。

Take the case of a couple, one of whom is fairly laid-back (and 'last minute', another characteristic of this type) and the other is more about being organized, when deciding on their next holiday.

以这样一对夫妇为例,面对即将到来的假期,一方的态度是顺其自然(做什么事情都喜欢拖延至最后一刻,这也是这个类型的人的另一个特点),而另一方则更加注重精确有序的安排。

The organized one starts planning a year in advance in order to get the best deal in the right location and wants certainty. The idea of leaving it to the last minute and risking not getting a flight is abhorrent.

有条理的一方会提前一年开始计划这次假期,以便自己能在最合适的地点买到最划算的东西。把事情拖到最后一分钟,冒着有可能赶不上飞机的风险,这种想法对于这类人来说是无法忍受的。

When the organized one asks the more laid-back one, in June **a year before** she has in mind to fix the holiday, where he would like to go on his holiday, he gives his reply on **his** time horizon, which is **this weekend**. The idea of trying to plan that much ahead is simply incomprehensible to the laid-back person and he considers his partner to be ridiculously over-organized, verging on 'OCD'.

早在六月份,也就是距离假期近一年的时间,做事有条理的妻子问生活比较散漫的丈夫,假期想去哪里度假,丈夫的回答却只是针对即将来临的假期,也就是本周末。对于懒散的人说,提前计划这么多事情简直是不可理喻,丈夫会觉得妻子有些过于谨慎了,甚至有些"强迫症"。

Getting them to agree to discuss a holiday, let alone arrive at an agreement will take some effort to avoid both getting stressed for very different reasons.

让他们坐下来讨论确定假期就已经很困难了,更不用说达成统一意见。生活态度的巨大差异,需要双方都做出一定的努力才能避免各方因为不同原因而疲惫。

Take the case of the executive with a more relaxed approach who is asked to prepare a report for Monday, the following week, this being Wednesday. She accepts the assignment and they agree delivery for Monday morning at 9.00 am.

以一个态度较为散漫的高管为例,在周三的这一天,她被要求在下周一的时候递交一份报告。她接受了这个任务,并答应会在下周一上午9点提交报告。

She thinks about the assignment in her head, realizes she will need quiet thinking time and decides she will complete it on Sunday afternoon.

她思考了报告内容,然后意识到自己需要安静的时间构思。因此,她决定在周日的下午完成它。

Her boss, the organized one, walks past her office on several occasions that same Wednesday and asks her how she is getting on; she says fine. Seeing no evidence of physical progress, he gets increasingly stressed. He cannot stop himself from regularly checking and gets more and more agitated.

她的老板,一个做事井井有条的人,在这周三几次经过她的办公室,并向她询问报告的进度,她的回答是没问题。由于看不到报告的进展,她的老板倍感压力。他不停地过去查看,并感到越来越焦虑。

Eventually, he goes in to see her and, now very stressed, asks her why she hasn't started, whether she intends to do the project after all or whether he should find someone else to complete it. She is surprised and hurt and wonders whether he believes her capable of undertaking the assignment. She says, with some barely concealed anger, that it will be ready on Monday morning *as agreed*.

最终,老板再次压力重重的走进她的办公室,问她为什么还不开始写报告,是不是想把这份工作交给其他人来完成。她感到震惊的同时又觉得很受伤,她现在不确定老板是否相信她可以如期完成这项任务。她带着几乎无法掩饰的怒气说,报告将会在下周一上午如期交付。

And it is and is perfectly done.

确实,她如期完成并交付了这份报告。

The issue is not one of competence but life style expectation. They have different life management needs and preferences, which affect how they see the world.

这里的问题不是她的能力,生活方式的差异。这位女高管和她的老板对生活方式有不同的需求和偏好,这也影响了他们看待事物的方式。

It is, as before, not about right and wrong. **It is all about understanding the other person and making appropriate *changes to one's own perception.***

这和上文提到的夫妇一样,不是关乎对错的问题,而是在于相互理解,并对自己的观点做出适当的改变。

Clearly if there had been a question of incompetence or laziness, the situation would have required different handling. But it was purely a question of life management and 'we all get to Christmas at the same time!'

显然,如果实际问题确实是因为能力不足或懒惰造成的,那么另当别论。但这纯粹是关乎生活态度管理的问题,毕竟最终我们都能得到一样的结果。

Under such circumstances there is no value whatever in trying to change someone else's preferences, even if that were possible. What is more important is to understand the differences, build new skills and adjust one's own behaviour accordingly.

在这种情况下,即使有可能,成功改变他人的偏好也是徒劳的。在这种情况下更重要的是了解彼此间的差异,培养自己的新技能,并适当地调整自己的行为习惯。

The secret of change is to focus your energy, not on fighting the old, but on building the new.
Dan Millman

做出改变的秘诀不是与旧习惯对抗,而是集中精力,尝试建立新的习惯。
丹·米尔曼

Empathy, warmth and sincerity

同理心、热情、真诚

The first four psychological characteristics have been on a continuum from one extreme to the other where none are either good or bad. They are simply preferences. The important factor is to understand the preference differences between individuals, what happens when they interact and how to manage them effectively.

前面讲述的四种心理特征是一个连续统一体,从一个极端延续到另外一个极端,它们没有好坏之分,只是每个人的偏好不同。重要的是要理解个体之间的偏好差异,当不同的个体进行互动时会发生什么,以及如何有效地进行管控。

The next two characteristics—empathy, warmth and sincerity and a sense of humour—are different in that low is less good than high.

接下来的两个特质便是同理心、热情和真诚,还有幽默感。它们的不同之处在于,在这些特质上水平高的人,在这方面的表现要优于水平较低的人。

Having high levels will increase the ability to establish good relationships, while having low levels will limit this capacity. It is therefore beneficial to understand how to improve and then learn and exercise in order to become more successful.

这些特质上的高水平会增强建立良好人际关系的能力,而低水平则会限制这种能力。因此,了解如何提高自己水平,并不断加以学习和实践,从而大大提高建立成功人际关系的几率是非常重要的。

Empathy is the ability and desire to understand and share another person's feelings from their perspective, to place oneself in their shoes and experience emotionally what they are experiencing. *Compassion* and *sympathy* are closely linked to empathy, and are feelings of care for someone in need and the desire to help them.

同理心是一种从他人的立场理解并分享对方感受的能力,使人能够设身处地的为他人着想,并能感同身受他人的处境。怜悯和同情心是与同理心紧密关联的两种情感,也是关爱他人的情感基础,由此产生帮助他人的愿望。

Studies have shown clearly that empathy and a higher EQ (emotional quotient) encourages the development of positive social relationships, the ability to relate to others, to establish effective rapport and to mediate.

有研究清楚地表明,同理心和较高的EQ(情商)有助于发展积极的社会关系、建立与他人的联系,以及建立有效、融洽关系,提高调解能力。

Children (and adults) can and should be helped and encouraged to learn to become more empathetic.

我们应当帮助和鼓励儿童(也包括成年人)学习如何变得更加有同理心。

This can be done by having them imagine themselves in the shoes of others (whether real cases or from stories) and learning to understand and identify their own feelings.

比如让他们想象自己站在别人的立场上(无论是从真实的案例还是故事中想象),学会理解和分析自己的感受。

Doing this subtly but regularly will help the child develop her sensitivity to others and enhance her care and consideration for others.

巧妙而有规律地进行这种练习,能够帮助孩子培养对他人的敏感性,增强小孩子对他人的关心和体贴。

Empathy is usually separated into **cognitive empathy**—the ability to understand another's perspective or mental condition (but not necessarily agree with it)—and **affective or emotional empathy**—the ability to be affected by another's emotional state and to respond appropriately.

同理心通常分为认知同理心(理解他人观点或心理状况的能力,但不一定同意)和情感同理心(受他人情绪状态影响并做出恰当反应的能力)。

Empathy is a skill that is, to a certain degree, innate, but which can also be learned and nurtured. Empathy gradually develops through life and is greatly enhanced by having experienced similar difficult situations, which increases greater empathic understanding.

在某种程度上来说,同理心是一种与生俱来的技能,但也可以通过后天学习和培养来获得。同理心在生活中逐渐发展,通过经历与他人类似的困境得到增强,大大提高共情理解。

Warmth—a sincere understanding and caring for others—invites and inspires trust, while *sincerity* creates a spontaneously authentic and truthful environment.

热情——一种对人真诚的理解和关爱——这种特质能够吸引并激发人与人之间的信任,而真诚待人则会有利于创造自然真实的人际环境。

Research has shown, in the case of counselling, that successful outcomes are not so much the result of the method of counselling but much more the result of the level of warmth, empathy and sincerity of the counsellor.

研究表明,在咨询行业,事情之所以取得成功并不是因为得到了合适的建议,而是咨询顾问的热情、同理心和真诚所带来的结果。

This indicates the extent to which all three together are vital to establish rapport and create positive relationships.

通向幸福的阶梯

这表明了三者在建立融洽积极的人际关系方面的重要性。

The higher the level of empathy, warmth and sincerity, the greater the ability to establish effective and fruitful relationships.

同理心、热情和真诚度的水平越高,建立有效、富有成果的人际关系能力就越强。

What are the best ways to demonstrate these every day?

在现代生活中,如何展示自己的这些特质呢?

1. Listen and pay attention.
1. 仔细倾听;

2. Make and hold eye contact.
2. 保保持眼神交流;

3. Find commonalities.
3. 寻找共同点;

4. Smile, especially when the other person smiles.
4. 微笑,特别是别人对你微笑的时候;

5. Be authentic, polite, supportive, uplifting, enthusiastic and kind.

5. 保持真实、礼貌待人、支持他人、积极向上、保持热情、心怀善意;

6. Take responsibility for actions.
6. 对对自己的行为负责;

7. Be prepared to be vulnerable.
7. 不掩饰自身的脆弱;

8. Trust, in order to be trusted.
8. 信任别人,才能被别人所信任;

9. Do not blame others.
9. 不要把错误归咎于别人。

Most of these are very obvious, but surprisingly difficult to do well, consistently and in differing or difficult situations.

其中大多数看起来都很容易做到,但要想在不同的场景或棘手的情况下始终保持却异常困难。

This is particularly the case in the high-speed, stressed and rushed environment in which we live. An environment that encourages selfishness over altruism ('I have no time to listen or help') and restricts the time available for what many may see as niceties but which are essentials to relationship building and obtaining positive results.

在我们所处的高速、紧张、匆忙的环境中更是如此。一个强调自私自利，忽略利他主义的环境(说着"我没时间听，没时间帮忙")，限制了许多人在细微之处上花费的时间，而这些细微之处正是建立良好的人际关系和获得积极结果的必要条件。

Listening and paying attention

仔细倾听

This list of possible actions to demonstrate empathy are largely self-explanatory.
Let us consider two very important ones in more detail:

上面列出的这个清单在很大程度上证明了同理心是一种不言自明的行为。
现在我们重点考虑下面这两个问题：

1. Listening and paying attention, and
1. 用心倾听

2. Establishing trust.
2. 建立信任

Listening and paying attention are much harder than usually imagined and yet in many respects are the most important of all.

用心倾听比我们想象得要困难的多,但在很多方面却是重中之重。

We have two ears and one mouth
so that we can listen twice as much as we speak.
An old proverb

上帝给人两只耳朵一张嘴,是为了要人多听少说。
古谚语

Sometimes we have so much we would like to transmit and we are so keen to get it all out in time lest we forget what we were going to say, that we fail to turn the receiver on.

我们有太多的东西需要表达。生怕自己忘了说什么,总是急切地一股脑地倒出来,但却忘了打开自己的接收键。

This is especially so for the high energy-high drive group and the results-based decision taker.

尤其是精力充沛和以结果为导向的决策者,更是如此。

There are three main ways to listen:

倾听主要有三种方式:

1. Listening to learn
1. 学习型倾听

2. Listening to evaluate
2. 评估型倾听

3. Listening openly
3. 开放型倾听

1. Listening to learn
1. 学习型倾听

Listening to learn happens in most daily activities, such as listening to the news or advice. A certain amount of concentration is required as well as some conscious effort—especially to quieten down our self-talk, which will try to interfere with our thinking process and disturb our concentration.

学习型倾听多发生在日常活动中,比如听新闻或别人提出的建议。需要一定的专注力和自我意识的努力,尤其要改善自我对话的情况,否则,我们的思维会被自我对话干扰,专注力也会被打乱。

This mode of listening is often associated with taking notes so as to be able to review the information later on.

这种倾听模式通常与记笔记联系在一起,方便以后能够对其加以复习。

When establishing or developing relationships, however, this type of listening is insufficient because the act of taking notes detracts from being able to listen completely. If you are writing, you cannot be listening at the same time.

然而,在关系的建立和发展阶段,这种模式的倾听是远远不够的,因为记笔记的行为会降低倾听的能力。在记笔记的时候,你不能同时集中精力去听。

2. Listening to evaluate
2. 评估型倾听

Listening to evaluate, also known as critical listening requires more concentration and effort than listening to learn, and is about making judgments and analysing detail.

评估型倾听,也被称为批判性倾听。相比学习型倾听,它需要更多的专注力和精力来判断和分析细节。

This entails an active engagement of the brain to decipher what is being said and to make assessments—'I like what I'm hearing'; 'This is very different from my own beliefs'; 'Why would the speaker think that?'; 'Where did that opinion come from?'

这就需要大脑的积极参与来破译别人的话,并对其作出评估——"我喜欢他刚刚说的话"、"这跟我个人的信仰大不相同"、"为什么他会这么想"、"这种观点从何而来?"。

Listening to evaluate is a very important way of learning as it requires the brain to take in information, compare it with other data previously stored and then make decisions and judgments.

评估型倾听是一种重要的学习方式,因为它需要大脑接收信息,并与之前存储的数据相比较,然后做出决定和判断。

It runs the risk, however, that we substitute our own opinions and biases for those of the person we are listening to.

然而,如果我们完全用自己的观点和偏见去理解讲话者时,也会产生一定的风险。

The efficiency of the learning process is impaired, especially if, at the same time, our self-talk is working overtime interjecting pre-judgements or prejudices.

学习过程的效率会因此受到阻碍,尤其是当我们自言自语地将自己的预先判断和偏见插入讲话者的观点时。

We cannot listen well if we think we already know.

如果我们认为自己已经足够了解一件事,就会丧失仔细倾听的能力

It is impossible for a person to begin to learn what he thinks he already knows.
Epictetus

一个人不可能学习他自认为已经掌握的知识。
埃皮克提图

3. Listening openly
3. 开放型倾听

The third way of listening, and the one that is most appropriate for establishing and building relationships, is to listen openly, also known as empathic or active listening.

第三种倾听的方式,也是最适合建立和发展人际关系的方式,即开放型倾听,也被称为同理心倾听或主动型倾听。

Listening openly means focusing one's entire being on what the other person is saying, without interruption, without judgment, without trying to find solutions, without allowing that inner voice to interfere and without giving advice.

开放型倾听意味着全神贯注地听对方讲话，不去打断，不去判断，也不会试图帮助对方找到解决方法，不会让自己内心的声音打扰对方，也不会给予任何建议。

The only objective is to understand properly what is being said and the emotions that lie behind. **It is listening with the innocence of the child and not the conviction of the adult.** Nothing else gets in the way.

唯一的目的是正确理解对方的讲话内容和隐藏在背后的情感。这个过程要带着孩子般的无邪去倾听，而不是带着成年人的世故去批判。完完全全不受到干扰。

When someone listens openly, their eyes open more widely (to absorb more information) and focus more intently on the speaker.

当一个人开放地倾听时，他的眼界会放大（以吸收更多的信息）并且更专注地倾听讲话的人。

They are taking in the information with their ears but also with their eyes and other senses in order to receive the greatest amount of data and interpret not only the words used, but often more importantly, nonverbal cues such as body language, facial expression, breathing, tone of voice and eye movement.

听者通过耳朵、眼睛和其它感官,最大程度地接收信息。解读语言表达的和那些来自肢体、面部、呼吸节奏、声音语调、眼动所表达的非语言暗示,而这些也往往是更重要的。

After the speaker has finished, the active, open listener may paraphrase what has been said, not with a view to agreeing or disagreeing (which would signify making a judgment) but to check that they have understood properly what is being said, to avoid misunderstanding and build trust.

当讲者说完后,积极、开放型的听者可能会转述他刚刚的讲话内容,他们这样做并不是为了表明自己是否赞同讲话者(赞同或反对都意味着做出判断),而是确保自己已经正确地理解了讲话内容,以免引起误解,难以建立起彼此间的信任。

If the listener paraphrases well, they have obviously been listening and an atmosphere of cooperation can start to be created.

如果听者能改述得很好,这说明他们确实一直在仔细地倾听讲者,而彼此间的合作也由此开始建立起来。

Building trust

建立信任

Trust has to be earned. It is not a right. It cannot be assumed. It cannot be requested. It takes time, patience, understanding and respect. It develops over time and becomes something very special shared between individuals. It is a fundamental building block of real friendship and happiness. It is a major key to establishing and keeping good relationships.

在人际交往中,信任是不可或缺的一部分。它不是一种权利,不是一种假设,也不是一种要求。信任的建立需要时间、耐心、理解和尊重,随着时间的推移而成长,成为个体间最特殊的共享。信任是获得真正的友谊和幸福的基石,是建立和保持良好关系的关键。

It can, however, be easily and quickly destroyed.

然而,却很容易被摧毁。

If you want to be trusted, be trustworthy. This means worthy of someone's trust.

如果你想被人信任,就要先把自己变成一个值得信赖的人。也就是说你值得被他人信任。

How is trust built and how does one become worthy of another's trust?

信任是如何建立的？怎样获得别人的信任？

Plato believed that in order to achieve happiness, human beings must be consciously moral and develop wisdom, courage, moderation and justice.

柏拉图认为，人类要想获得幸福，就要先遵守道德，培养自己的智慧、勇气，克制自己的欲望，寻求正义。

Aristotle believed that this required not just reflection but also action. It needed to be practised every day.

亚里士多德则认为这需要人不断地反思和行动，也需要每天持之以恒地训练。

Wisdom and justice encompass and depend on trust.

智慧和正义包含并取决于信任。

Trustworthy people have the following characteristics.

值得信赖的人都拥有以下特征：

通向幸福的阶梯　　　269

1. They are honest. They do not lie, steal or mislead. They are straightforward, do not manipulate or seek to control.
1. 诚实。不会说谎、偷窃或误导他人。直截了当,不操纵或试图掌控他人。

2. They have integrity and respect for all people, whatever their background, belief, colour or creed.
2. 为人正直,尊重所有人,拥有不同的文化背景、宗教信仰和肤色。

3. They are loyal to friends and family. They help and support them unselfishly in times of need. They cherish and nurture them in their growth and praise them in their successes. They defend them against gossip and negative talk.
3. 忠于朋友和家人。在朋友和家人需要的时候,无私地给予他们帮助和支持。珍惜并呵护朋友、家人的成长,为他们的成功而喝彩,保护他们不受流言蜚语和负面言论的伤害。

4. Their word is their bond. When they make a promise, they keep it.
4. 言而有信。承诺的事就一定会做到。

5. They are dependable. When they undertake a task, they deliver and can be relied on to do the right thing.
5. 可靠。如期完成任务,并可以正确地处理问题。

6. They keep the confidences and secrets that others entrust to them.
6. 为他人保守秘密。

7. They are gentle with other's feelings.
7. 温柔待人。

8. They are not afraid to say they are wrong or that they do not know. They are not afraid of change.
8. 不惧怕承认错误或承认自己对某事物不了解，也不害怕改变。

9. They seek the truth and inspire confidence.
9. 寻求真理并以此激发自信。

> *If someone is able to convince me and show me that what I do or think is not right, I will gladly change; for I seek the truth, by which no one was ever injured.*
> **Marcus Aurelius**

如果有人能够说服我，让我知道我所想或所做的是错误的，我会很乐意改变；因为我寻求真理，没有人会因为寻求真理而受伤。
马可·奥勒留

A sense of humour

幽默感

Humour is a wonderful stress reliever. It lightens the atmosphere and defuses potentially tense situations. Laughter is a great healer and rejuvenates the soul.

幽默是一种很好的解压方式,能缓和气氛,化解紧张局势。开怀大笑是一种很好的治疗方法,能使灵魂恢复活力。

It requires subtlety, sensitivity, good listening and observation skills, a way with words and courage. It should only be used in the right situation and with the right audience—to not cause offence.

幽默感需要细腻、敏锐、良好的倾听和观察能力,兼顾了言语和勇气。幽默感仅应该在正确的场合,对合适的听众使用—以避免冒犯他人

Having a sense of humour helps establish and maintain good relationships, but only if done well.

幽默感有利于建立和保持良好的人际关系,但前提是要合理运用。

This is not about the ability to tell jokes and it is absolutely not about doing so at others' expense. It is about finding what is amusing in a situation, however silly, and laughing together at it—together. The experience is uplifting for all.

幽默感与讲笑话的能力无关，也不是以消费他人为代价。而是在某个情景中，发现某个傻傻的，却又令人感觉有趣的点，让大家一起开怀大笑。这个过程让所有人都能眼前一亮、提振气氛。

People who can laugh at themselves become more vulnerable to others, which increases their own humanity and attractiveness. They show that they do not take themselves too seriously and are thus more likely to be better companions.

自嘲的人更容易在情绪上感染别人，同时也增加了他们的人格魅力和吸引力。他们的这种"不拿自己当回事儿"，使他们更有可能成为一位优秀的伴侣。

This also build their resilience because, when problems occur, they can see the lighter side, have a better perspective and are better able to let go negative feelings and move on.

幽默感也能增强人的适应挫折的能力。遇到问题时，这类人能看到更光明的一面，拥有更广阔的视角，更能放下消极情绪，继续前行。

I've also regarded a sense of humour as one of the most important things on a big expedition. When you're in a difficult or dangerous situation, or when you're depressed about the chances of success, someone who can make you laugh eases the tension.
Edmund Hillary

我把幽默感视为探险中最重要的事情之一。
当你面对困难或陷入危险的境地，当你为丧失成功的机会而沮丧时，能让你笑起来的人，
便可以缓解紧张情绪。
埃德蒙·希拉里

Laughing at the same jokes or the same situations also creates a connection with another person and a common bond, helping to build a stronger, more intimate relationship.

因为同样的笑话或身在同一个处境而大笑也能建立起与他人的联系和共同的纽带，有助于发展一种更牢固、更亲密的关系。

Imagination was given to a man to compensate him for what he is not. A sense of humour to console him for what he is.

> 人之所以有想象力，就是用来弥补他所
> 没有的东西；人之所以有幽默感，
> 就是为了让他接受原本的自己。

Having a sense of humour requires creativity in finding the right words to deliver a clever witticism, an amusing repartee or a juxtaposed, surprising image.

想要培养幽默感，就要创造性地找到合适的词语来巧妙地表达一种诙谐、有趣的回答或建立一种并列的、令人讶异的形象。

It means having the ability to see that much of life is absurd and random and to draw comic inferences and incongruous images whose surreal quality amuse by their very absurdity. Spontaneous creativity creates ideas that delight.

这是一种能看到生活中荒诞和随机性的能力，并从中得出抽离出荒谬的推论和不相称的画面。而正是因为它如此无稽，使得这个超现实的画面充满趣味性。毫无预备的创造性激发出令人愉悦的想法。

Sometimes the simplest situations can amuse, but it is only the people with a sense of humour who will laugh.

有时最简单的清醒也能引人发笑,但只有拥有幽默感的人才能明白它的笑点。

In order to develop a sense of humour, watch humourous programmes, listen to amusing podcasts, look for cartoons in the papers, read funny books and go to comedies at the theatre.

观看幽默节目、收听妙语连珠的播客、阅读报纸上的漫画板块或妙趣横生书籍、看幽默小品和喜剧表演,这些都能培养幽默感。

By immersing oneself in humour, humour becomes part of the soul. This cannot help but enhance one's sense of humour.

沉浸在幽默的情绪中,幽默就会变成灵魂的一部分。这也在无形中增强了一个人的幽默感。

A sense of humour, once develops, is forever.

幽默感一旦形成,便永久存在。

***You don't stop laughing when you grow old,
you grow old when you stop laughing.***

真正的变老是从你不再开怀大笑开始的。

Mirroring

镜像模仿

Having now examined some characteristics or traits of what 'looks like me' might mean for our subconscious mind, it is clear that this is a very complex subject, easily prone to misinterpretation and error, which is why so many relationships are, at best, lukewarm.

现在我们已经研究了"和我最像"这个特质对潜意识的意义。很明显,这是一个非常复杂的问题,容易产生误解和错误。也正因此才会有那么多不冷不热的关系。

When people who have very different preferences and characteristics meet up, the likelihood of disharmony will be very high as they will see themselves as coming from different planets.

当有着截然不同的偏好和特征的人相遇时,产生不和谐的可能性非常高,他们会觉得自己和对方仿佛是来自两个星球的人。

The subconscious mind of the individuals concerned, while seeking to find its mirror image, will most likely not have the skills to adjust well to the differences encountered and the exchange ends up in discord and creates an unsatisfactory relationship.

相关个体的潜意识寻找自己的镜像时,很可能无法很好地适应所遇到的差异和分歧,交流最终以不和谐告终,留下令人不甚满意的关系。

One often hears the phrase 'I keep making the same mistake,' and this is in significant part because the person has not been exposed to or learnt the subtleties of the different characteristics described—let alone how to manage them.

我们时常听到这样一句话"我总是在犯同样的错误",这在很大程度上是因为这个人没有接触过或了解过拥有不同特征的微妙之处—更不用说如何管理这些差异。

They may think, again and again, that they have found the perfect friend, colleague or partner, only to realize subsequently the huge differences that exist between them. They were not looking with the right eyes at the right things.

他们可能会一次又一次地认为自己找到了完美的朋友、同事或搭档,然后一次又一次地意识到他们之间原来存在着巨大的差异。他们没有能力找到症结所在。

Another common phrase is 'opposites attract'. The reality is very different. People may think they are attracted to their 'opposite' when, in reality, on the six characteristics described above, their deep attachment is to people similar to themselves. They have not understood what the important elements are and why what they consider to be 'differences' are actually only variations of the same trait.

另外一个常见的短语是"反向吸引",但现实情况却与之大相径庭。人们也许认为自己是被"与自己相反的"所吸引,但实际上,在以上所描述的六个特征中,人对与自己相似的人有着深刻的依恋。说自己被"反向吸引"的人,其实还没有懂得他们之间重要的元素是哪些,也没意识到,其实他们所认为的"差异"只是同一特质的变异而已。

With our newfound knowledge of some of these traits, let us now examine the concept and power of 'mirroring'.

随着我们对其中一些特征的新发现,现在让我们研究一下"镜像"的概念和它的力量。

People will be more trustful of those with whom they feel a natural affinity and less trustful of those who seem different. This is the basis of all human prejudice.

人会更加信任那些和他们有天然亲近感的人,而不那么信任那些看起来与自己不同的人。这是人类所有偏见的基础。

In order to have the best possible chance of establishing a relationship of trust with another person who seems, on the surface, to be different, we need not to try to change them but to change ourselves to be more like them.

为了尽可能有机会与表面上看起来与自己不同的人建立信任关系，我们不需要改变他们，而是试图改变自己，让自己看起来和他们更相似。

Mirroring means observing the other person's body language, tone of voice, speed of speech, breathing, language and words used and beliefs and then adjusting our own behaviour to more closely match that of the other person.

镜像模仿指的是观察对方的肢体语言、讲话语调及语速、呼吸节奏、常用语言和用词以及观点，然后调整自己，在这些方面变得更接近对方的行为。

This has to be done sensitively and subtly.

要做到细微但又不刻意。

The objective, and the only objective, is to establish a good relationship with someone else **by making efforts to see, feel and interpret the world through their eyes and thus create a connection.**

我们的目的,这么做唯一的目的,就是努力从他/她的视角去看、去感受、去解读这个世界,从而和这个人找到感觉,建立一种良好的关系。

If this sounds like gross manipulation it isn't—for several reasons.

听起来像是操纵他人的粗鄙行为,但事实并非如此——原因有多种。

People see through manipulation very quickly and if the approach is not authentic the attempt at mirroring will fail.

以操纵他人为目的是很容易被别人看穿的;如果实践起来不够真实,镜像模仿就会失败。

Genuine mirroring requires paying close attention and listening carefully to what the other person is saying and feeling. This cannot be done well if the one mirroring is self-absorbed or has an ulterior motive.

真诚的镜像模仿需要仔细关注、仔细聆听对方所说的话和感受。如果镜像中的那个人只顾自己,或者别有用心,那就无法做到仔细关注和仔细聆听。

Mirroring cannot be faked and the surprising thing is that, while the person being mirrored may start off as a stranger, the act of mirroring will make them seem 'more like me' to my subconscious mind *as I continue to alter my own behaviour.*

镜像模仿是假装不出来的。奇怪的是,尽管被镜像的人一开始可能是一个陌生人,但当我们不断改变自己的行为时,镜像的行为会让我们的潜意识觉得他们"更像我"。

The very act of listening actively and observing carefully is a welcome signal of consideration.

积极倾听和仔细观察这两个行为本身就是一种关心他人的举动。

Matching body posture, intensity and rhythm of speech, use of words and philosophical beliefs (unless they are objectionable for any reason) creates a state of agreement with the other person and the other person's subconscious will respond positively to the attention shown.

主动去配合另一个人的身体姿态、说话强度和节奏、常用语和个人信仰(除非是无可救药地令人反感)会创造出一种与对方一致的状态,而对方的潜意识则会对其所接收到的注意力给予积极的回应。

An understanding of neuro-linguistic programming (NLP) is of help here. The words used and the feelings demonstrated by a person are a strong indicator of that person's 'code', of how they subjectively and consciously experience the world and the verbal and non-verbal communication patterns they use to do so.

这里,稍微提一下神经语言程序学(NLP)能帮助大家更好地理解。一个人所使用的词语和所表现出来的情感是破解他"代码"的指示器,从中,可以了解他是如何主观地、有意识地体验这个世界,以及他用哪些言语和非言语沟通模式来体验和表达。

If a person experiences the world primarily through visual images, they will use words which have visual connotations, such as, 'Do you see what I mean?' and create vivid images.

如果一个人主要通过视觉图像来体验世界,他会使用一些具有视觉内涵的词汇,比如,[1](类似这样,能够创造出一幅生动的画面的词。

If they are more attuned to receiving their signals about the world through *sound*, they will use words with auditory connotations, 'How does that sound to you?'

---

[1] 原文为"Do you see what I mean?" 英文中"see"在这里有明白的意思,同时作为动词,see的本意是"看"。

如果他们更习惯于通过声音接收世界的信号,他们会使用带有听觉内涵的词汇,比如:"这样听起来怎么样?"[2]

If they are primarily kinaesthetic in their subjective subconscious experience, they will use words of feeling and tactile sensations, 'How do you *feel* about that?'

如果他们的主观潜意识体验是以动觉型(kinaesthetic)为主,他们就会使用感觉和触觉型的词语进行表达,"你(对此)感觉怎么样?"

A person whose code is VAK (visual, auditory, kinaesthetic, in that order) will enjoy using imaginative language and images but will most likely not like touching.

如果一个人的代码是VAK(按照视觉、听觉、动觉的顺序排列),他会偏向于使用富有想象力的语言和图像来表达,但很可能不太喜欢使用触觉型的词语。

A person whose code is AKV will respond best to soft melodious tones and voices, not strident ones, and will be less impressed with grand imaginative tableaus.

2　原文为"How does that sound to you?"意为"你觉得如何?"而这里的"觉得"用了"sound"来表达,"sound"本意有"听起来"的意思。

如果一个人的代码是AKV（按照听觉、动觉、视觉的顺序排列），那么他对柔和悦耳的旋律和声音最为敏感，不会喜欢尖锐刺耳的声音，而且对于宏大的、富有想象力的画面也不会太感冒。

A person whose code is KVA will like to feel, sense and touch but may not be so good at listening.

如果一个人的代码是KVA（按照动觉、视觉、听觉的顺序排列），他会比较喜欢使用感官或触觉，但可能不太擅长倾听。

Of course this is a gross oversimplification, but it does provide another insight into how people view the world and another tool by which to achieve successful mirroring.

当然，这只是一种粗略的过度简化的解读，但确实为我们提供了看待世界的另一种视角，以及实现成功镜像模仿的另一种方法。

In the same way as we examined the potential issues that result from people's differing energy, thought processes, decision-making and lifestyle needs, so too, we need to assess the issues that result from their differing NLP characteristics.

和我们研究人的精力、思维过程、决策方式和生活态度来解决的差异问题一样，我们也需要评估因为不同的NLP（神经语言程序学）特征所导致的问题。

If people with very different NLP profiles want to establish good relationships, they will need to be aware of and adjust to these differences.

如果在NLP（神经语言程序学）配置方面大不相同的人想要建立良好的关系，他们都需要有意识地不断调整，适应这种差异。

For example, a primarily kinaesthetic person will respond best to words and behaviours that appeal to the senses. They will enjoy physical closeness, holding hands, touching and feeling. They need to feel and touch their universe.

例如，一个以动觉型为主的人会对感官型的词语和行为比较敏感，他们会享受身体上的亲密，如牵手、触摸和其它感觉官能。对他们来说，需要用感受和触摸来与外界进行交流和沟通。

If their partner has a low kinaesthetic sense, they will find this uncomfortable, as if something is missing, as if they are unable to show their true caring and loving self. They will view their partner as somewhat cold and unreceptive. To them feeling and touching are prime signals of warmth and togetherness.

如果他们的伴侣动觉性较低,他们会对此很介意,感觉好像缺失了什么,自己无法感受到对方的关心和爱意。他们会认为对方有些冷漠和不善接受。对于他们而言,感觉和触摸是热情和团聚的主要信号。

On the other hand, a primarily visual person with a low kinaesthetic sense will be uncomfortable with touching or holding hands, preferring visual clues such as being well groomed, properly turned out, clean and attractive to the eye.

另一方面,一个以视觉型为主,而动觉性较低的人对触摸和牵手比较抵触,他们更喜欢视觉型的线索,如穿着得体、妆容整洁、引人注目等。

In order to find happiness, they will need to discuss openly their differing needs and reactions and learn how to develop all their senses. If they are to be happy together, they will want to learn how all their senses can be nurtured to please their partner. This will not only make them open to new sensations but also create positive energy and enhance inner well-being.

为了寻求幸福,他们需要开诚布公地讨论各自的需求和反应,学习如何全面开发自己的感官。如果他们想要在一起愉快地生活,就要学习如何培养自己所有的感官来取悦自己的伴侣。这不仅会让他们体验到前所未有的感觉,也会创造出积极的能量,增强内在幸福感。

Mirroring enables people to understand more effectively what motivates and stimulates others and thus serves to establish good relationships with almost anyone.

镜像模仿让人更加有效地理解他人受到哪些动力和激励,从而有助于与他人,甚至可以说与任何人建立良好的关系。

This is an enriching and happy experience and the basis for widening one's circle of friends, as well as learning more broadly and more completely.

这是一段充实而快乐的经历,也是扩大交际圈,并更广泛、更全面进行学习的基础。

Letting go

放手

In creating, maintaining and nurturing excellent relationships (as well as living a less stressful life) it is important to recognize the importance of being able to 'let go'.

在创造、维持和培养良好的人际关系(或过一种低压力生活)地过程中,认识到能够"放手"的重要性是非常必要的。

Letting go, a key Stoic philosophy, means we acknowledge our limitations when it comes to our relationships and that we cannot change things we cannot control or seek to change people.

放手,是斯多葛学派的一项重要哲学。它意味着我们承认自己在人际关系上的局限性,承认我们无法改变哪些自己无法控制,无法改变他人。

If we try to do this, we will only inevitably become frustrated and angry and may in fact promote the opposite of what we are seeking to achieve. We also reduce our self-esteem.

如果不懂放手,只会不可避免地变得沮丧和愤怒,还很可能事与愿违。同时,也会降低自己的自尊心。

Any person capable of angering you becomes your master; he can anger you only when you permit yourself to be disturbed by him.

任何能激怒你的人都会成为你的主人;
只有你允许自己被他打扰时,你才会感到愤怒。

For example, when we are communicating with a colleague by text or email, and are in a hurry, if we do not receive a quick reply, how do we react? How do we interpret the lack of response? And what do we then do?

例如,在时间很紧急的情况下,我们通过短信或电邮与同事进行沟通,但并没有得到及时的回复,该怎么办呢?我们该如何解读对方的没有反应这件事?我们该怎么做?

Unless we are able to let go—because we cannot control the response—we will quite probably start to think 'something's not right.' Maybe the other party is ignoring us. Maybe they no longer wish to talk to us. Maybe they are not well. Maybe, maybe, maybe. Before long we start imagining the worst.

除非我们能够选择放手(因为我们无法控制别人的反应),不然的话,我们很可能会开始思考"有什么不对劲的地方"。也许对方忽视了我们,也许他们不想再和我们进行任何交流,也许对方病了。也许这个,也许那个。然后我们就开始考虑可能出现的最糟糕的情况。

And yet, in the vast majority of instances, there is a simple and innocent reason for the delay. The other person had just jumped into a car to go to their next appointment. Their next meeting had just started and they were unable to respond immediately. They had other more urgent messages to deal with. They had to go and pick up the children.

只可惜,在大多数情况下,没有及时回复的原因,其实是"简单"且"单纯"的。也许对方刚刚上车准备赴约,也许会议才刚刚开始,对方无法立刻做出回复,也许对方有更紧急的信息要先处理,也许对方要去接小孩放学。

We attribute, quite unnecessarily, motives and feelings to what were purely imagined occurrences. Our inherent fears, stimulated by our subconscious mind and previous experience, overwhelm our sense of reality.

我们把动机和感情完全归因于纯属想象的事件,而这是完全不必要的。我们内在的恐惧,被自己的潜意识和过往的经验刺激到,压倒了对现实的感觉。

> ***We suffer more often in imagination than in reality.***
> **Seneca**

我们在想象中所遭受的苦痛要远远大于现实生活。
塞内卡

If we had simply let go, because we cannot (and should not) control the actions of another, then we would have avoided the frustration, stress and even anger caused by our perception of the situation.

如果知道自己不能(也不应该)控制他人的行为,于是简单地选择放手,那么我们就可以避免因对形势的感知而产生的沮丧、压力甚至愤怒。

And if we had continued to bombard them with more texts, we would have risked angering them and worsening the problem—all quite unnecessarily.

反之,如果我们继续用更多的短信来轰炸对方,只会激怒他们,使问题进一步恶化,非常没有必要。

If you are distressed by anything external, the pain is not due to the thing itself, but rather to your estimate of it; and this you have the power to revoke at any moment.
Marcus Aurelius

你的痛苦不是来源于外界事物,
而是来自于你对它的想象,而你可以随时停止对它的
想象来消除你的痛苦。
马可·奥勒留

If we want our relationships to thrive, we need to learn to let go by saying to ourselves that anything we cannot control is OK and we'll move on.

如果我们想要拥有亲密无间的关系,就要学会放手。告诉自己脱离我们掌控的事情并不是问题,我们能做的就是继续前行。

Once we have decided to let go, because it's OK, our insecurities diminish to the point of non-existence. What could have resulted in a serious misunderstanding and a damaged relationship has been avoided.

既然无法掌控是可以接受的，那么一旦选择放手，我们的不安全感就会消失，就此也避免了可能因此而产生严重误解和关系受损。

We have to develop the inner power to decide to let go and thus eliminate the control that outside events would otherwise have on us.

我们培养自己适时放手的内在力量，从而消除外界事物对我们的影响和控制。

You have power over your mind—not outside events. Realize this and you will find strength.

你的思想掌握在你自己手中，而不是由外界来控制。意识到这一点，你就会找到内在的力量。

However close a relationship with another, we should always acknowledge, respect and celebrate the fact that there are two separate people with separate identities, needs and wants.

无论与他人的关系有多么密切，我们都要认识到、尊重并欣赏这个事实：即两个不同的人，有着不同的认知、需求和欲望。

Some people, for various psychological reasons usually acquired in childhood, have greater need for, say, reassurance, praise, certainty, control or perfection. They, most of all, need to learn to let go, because they are most at risk of displaying the stressed reactions that can be so disruptive.

有些人，由于某些在童年时期已经存在的心理原因，对慰藉、赞扬、确定性、控制和完美有着更高的要求。这个群体中的大部分人都需要学会放手，因为他们对压力所表现出的反应可能会更具破坏性。

This is where letting go is vital but also most difficult.

也正是因为这个原因，放手如此重要却又难以做到。

Problems will arise if their needs swamp the one who does not have such requirements. If they need to be constantly in charge or have everything just right or be frequently recognized even for relatively trivial matters, it will overwhelm the other, and the relationship will inevitably falter.

如果个人在这些方面需求让没有这些需求的另一方感

到压力倍增,就会出现问题。如果一方需要不间断地掌控全局,或者要求一切都不出差错,或者即便是特别琐碎的事情也要得到对方的认可,这对另一方来说是窒息性的,他们的关系也会不可避免地被动摇。

This is especially so if accompanied by a desire to know everything all the time—another expression of control, which leads to constant and stressful questioning both of self and the other.

尤其是在一方总是想要知道所有的事情(这也是控制的一种表达),会导致对自我和他人持续不断的的质疑,让彼此压力倍增。

In many ways, letting go is an effective form of anti-stress therapy because, practised regularly, it enables the mind to avoid negative emotional responses such as anxiety and anger and helps develop and nurture strong and lasting relationships.

在很多事情上,放手是一种有效的抗压疗法。经常性地实践,能帮助大脑避免消极的情绪反应,如焦虑和愤怒,并有助于发展和培养强大和持久的关系。

Letting go also protects in times of real difficulties because it instils a sense of acceptance, and a calmer call to action, while avoiding the trauma of a single major aspiration, ambition or relationship going wrong.

放手也能在面对真正的困难时起到保护作用,它强调接受现实,以及一种更冷静的态度采取行动,同时还能避免因孤注一掷的期望、梦想或人际关系破裂后所带来的创伤。

It is sometimes also useful to remember that we are on this earth for a very short time and the little things that frustrate and annoy us are really of no significance compared to the enormous injustices that exist in the world.

有时只要想一下,我们在这个世界上只会存在极其短暂的一段时间,那些使我们感到沮丧和烦恼的事情,和世界上所存在的巨大的不公正相比,实在是微不足道。

We should live each day as if it is our last. We should thus think, do and be good while we can. All our relationships will benefit from this.

我们应该把生命中的每一天都当作最后一天来度过。因此,我们应该在所有力所能及的时候,去思考,去行动,去行善。我们所有的关系都会因此而受益。

We must be willing to get rid of the life we've planned, so as to have the life that is waiting for us.
Joseph Campbell

只有心甘情愿放弃精心策划的生活,
我们才能拥抱前方翘首以待的人生。
约瑟夫·坎贝尔

Letting go all else, cling to the following few truths. Remember than man lives only in the present, in this fleeting instant: all the rest of his life is either past and gone, or not yet revealed. This mortal life is a little thing, lived in a little corner of the earth: and little too is the longest fame to come, dependent as it is on a succession of fast-perishing little men who have no knowledge even of their own selves, much less of one long dead and gone.
Marcus Aurelius

抛开世俗的一切,只专注于以下真理。记住,人只活在当下。在这稍纵即逝的一瞬间,他的余生要么已经逝去,要么还未显现。凡人的生命是这尘世间微不足道的一件小事,即使是流芳百世的名声最终的归宿也是渺不足道的,因为它的传颂依赖于甚至都不了解自我的、即将逝去的一连串的小人物,更不用说一个早已亡故的人了。

马可·奥勒留

Love

爱

This section on the happiness of relationships would not be complete without a final word on the overwhelming importance of love.

如果没有阐述"爱"的重要性,那么幸福关系的这一章节是不完整的。

Amor vincit omnia—Love conquers all.

Amor vincit omnia—爱能征服一切。

All the advice provided in this section is to help to create the circumstances in which happy relationships can be created, unhappy relationships corrected and love can flourish.

本节所提供的所有建议都是为了帮助创造一种,可以建立幸福的关系,纠正痛苦的关系,并使爱意愈渐浓厚的环境。

Love is a deep feeling of affection of one person for another. It is always personal and individual.

爱是一个人对另一个人的深厚感情,并因人而异。

When people talk of loving a group of people or a family, they mean loving each individual person separately as a unique and complete human being.

别人说他们爱一个群体或一个家庭时,他们的意思是是爱其中的每一名成员,并把每一个成员视为一个完整独立的个体去爱。

The absence of a loved one compresses the heart and it aches. Expecting the return of a loved one creates longing and the warm glow of expectation. Being with a loved one eliminates the concept of time, as it ceases to exist.

爱人的离去会让人心痛不已,而对所爱之人归来的期待会让他们充满信心和希望。与相爱的人在一起,会让他们忘却时间的流逝,仿佛时间不存在般。

Romantic love is also about passion and sexual desire and these strong emotional feelings are wonderfully and perfectly normal and truly beneficial expressions of mutual enjoyment and happiness.

浪漫的爱情是由激情和性欲组成的,这些强烈的情感表现是非常正常且有益的表达方式,也是双方享受幸福的真正表现。

Romantic love alone, however blissful, is not enough to sustain a loving relationship over time. Love has to be nurtured by much deeper, subtler, more complex and longer-lasting expressions of devotion.

浪漫的爱情,无论有多么幸福,都无法维系长久的爱情关系。爱情的维系需要更深刻、更细致、更复杂和更长久的付出。

Love, which is encompassed by all the guidance provided so far, is about:

截止到这一章节,我们所提出的关于爱情的建议包括:

1. unconditional affection, understanding and acceptance
1. 无条件的关怀、理解和接受

2. responsibility, patience and letting go any ideas of control
2. 责任心、耐心以及放下掌控一切的欲望

3. unselfish devotion and dedication
3. 无私地奉献和付出

4. confidence and dependence
4. 自信和依赖

5. gentleness, kindness and warmth
5. 温柔、善良和热情

6. wanting rather than needing
6. 不苛求,顺其自然

7. giving and receiving
7. 给予和接受

8. nurturing and protecting
8. 培养和保护

Love hinders death. Love is life. … Love is God,
and to die means that I, a particle of love,
shall return to the general and eternal source.
Leo Tolstoy

爱能阻止死亡的到来。爱就是生活…爱就是上帝,而
死亡意味着我将化作爱的微粒,
回到普遍和永恒的源头。
列夫·托尔斯泰

Love is patient, love is kind. It does not envy,
it does not boast, it is not proud. It is not rude,
it is not self-seeking. It is not easily angered;
it keeps no record of wrongs. Love does not delight
in evil, but rejoices with the truth.
It always protects, always trusts, always hopes,
and always perseveres. Love never fails.
1 Corinthians 13:4–8

爱是恒久忍耐,又有恩慈,爱是不嫉妒,
爱是不自夸,不张狂,不做害羞的事,不求自己的益处,
不轻易发怒,不计算人的恶,不喜欢不义,只喜欢真
理;凡事包容,凡事相信,
凡事盼望,凡事忍耐;爱是永不止息。
哥林多前书第13章4-8节

In the end these things matter most:
How well did you love? How fully did you live?
How deeply did you let go?
Jack Kornfield writing about Buddhist ideas

归根结底最重要的是：你的爱有多深刻？
你活得有多充实？你放手的程度有多高？
杰克·柯恩菲德谈佛教

Love is the energizing elixir of the universe,
the cause and effect of all harmonies.
Anon

爱是宇宙能量的灵丹妙药，爱是所有和谐的因果。
佚名

It should now be evident that we have arrived at the last step, the happiness of harmony.

现在，我们终于来到了最后一个阶梯，和谐的幸福。

THE FIFTH STEP:
THE HAPPINESS OF HARMONY

第五步：和谐带来的幸福感

The fifth step, the happiness of harmony, comprises the best of all the previous steps: the intense feelings of happiness when achieving something difficult; the joy of helping another and giving of oneself; and the deeply personal and warm, intimate sense of affection and love from personal relationships.

第五步，和谐的幸福，它所带来的幸福感要高于前四个阶段，即排除万难取得成绩的强烈幸福感；帮助他人、奉献自己的喜悦感；个人关系中强烈、温暖、亲密的感情和爱情。

The results of an extensive international study showed a clear cross-cultural trend for considering happiness in terms of inner peace and harmony, with two powerful contextual factors. The first was associated with good relationships and the second with physical health.

一项广泛的国际研究结果表明,从内心平静与和谐的角度来看待幸福感是一种明显的跨文化趋势,它包含两个重要的情景因素。一个是良好的人际关系,另一个是身体健康。

Good relationships satisfy a critical psychosocial need to be known and valued, and this comes from having excellent relationships with family, friends and the communities in which we live. But is this enough for inner peace and the harmony of the soul?

良好的人际关系满足了一个关键心理需求,那就是我们需要被了解和被重视的需求。这一点主要来自于与家人、朋友和我们所生活的社区。 但是,这是否足以让人达到内心平静、心灵和谐呢?

True inner peace and harmony is much more complex, much more difficult to achieve and requires a much deeper examination and understanding.

达到真正的内心平静、心灵和谐要复杂得多,而且很难实现,它需要更深层次的自我审视和理解。

Before we can achieve true inner peace and harmony we need to be able to perceive, with total clarity and honesty, the good and the bad around us and appreciate how we react to it, as well as the good and the bad in ourselves and how we manage, address or ignore that.

要真正达到内心平静、心灵和谐,我们要能够清晰、诚实地去认识周围事物的好与坏,并接受我们自己如何面对这些好与坏。同样,我们也需要清楚地认识到自己身上的好与坏,知道自己是如何管控、处理,又或者忽视自己这些问题的。

The happiness of harmony cannot exist if we choose to block out or conveniently ignore what is around us or inside us.

如果我们选择逃避或忽视那些周围或自身存在的问题,和谐的幸福就不可能存在。

How often do we choose to ignore the suffering that we experience around us or the disharmony that we experience internally when things don't go our way, when we are angry, anxious, frustrated, stressed or just sad? We simply allow these emotions to flood us without any consideration as to their real cause or effect. We do not take the time to examine properly the cause of our disquiet, what has given rise to it, whether it is justified or what lessons we might learn.

通向幸福的阶梯

每当事情不如人意，或者每次感到生气、焦虑、沮丧、压力或仅仅是伤心难过的时候，我们有多少次选择忽视周遭的痛苦或我们内心所经历的不和谐？相反，我们只是任由这些情绪泛滥，毫不考虑导致它们出现的真正原因或后续影响。也没有花时间正确地审视我们烦恼的根源，思考它的出现是否合理，又或者我们可以从中学到什么经验教训。

Buddhist teaching recognizes that the causes of disquiet need to be considered carefully and that life entails external and internal suffering. This is part of the human condition. To be alive is to experience suffering—at least at times. Without suffering there is no true understanding of life or a capacity to experience its opposite, joy.

佛教认为，我们需要仔细审视烦恼出现的原因，人活着就会有各种来自外界或内心的痛苦。这是人生的一部分，活着就是经历苦难-至少在某些时候就是这样。没有痛苦，就没有对生活的真正理解，也就没有能力体验痛苦的对立面—-快乐。

Attempts to block out, ignore or banish suffering from the mind will ultimately fail and cause further disharmony of the soul.

试图逃避、忽视或消除内心的痛苦终会失败，并会导致灵魂愈加不和谐。

Blocking out suffering is known to create mental disorders, such as that experienced by those who have suffered severe trauma, if they are unable to face, let alone process, their experiences.

众所周知,那些经历过严重创伤的人,如果他们不能直面曾经的伤口(更不用说消化那段经历),那么这种将痛苦拒之门外的行为将会导致精神障碍的发生。

> ***Buddhism teaches us not to try to run away from suffering. You have to confront suffering. You have to look deeply into the nature of suffering in order to recognize its cause, the making of the suffering.***
> **Thich Nhat Hanh**

> 佛家教导我们不要试图逃避苦难。
> 你必须直面痛苦,深入观察痛苦的本质,
> 才能认识到它的因,即痛苦的来源。
> 一行禅师

To achieve the happiness of harmony, we have to come to terms with the inescapable fact that life is not just about joy but also about suffering. We then have to learn to accept and manage this fundamental truth. We have to learn to understand our own consciousness and develop compassion as part of our quest for inner peace. Compassion enables us to handle suffering.

通向幸福的阶梯

为了视线和谐的幸福,我们必须认识到这样一个不可争辩的事实:即活着不仅仅是享受快乐,也要忍受痛苦。我们必须学会理解和承认这一基本真理。在寻求内心平静的道路上,我们要学会理解自我意识和培养同情心。同情与怜悯让我们能度过苦难。

To develop our own consciousness in a way that can foster inner peace and mental harmony, we have to learn to be true to ourselves. We have to consciously and deliberately do our best to learn wisdom, compassion and justice, while helping to protect, heal and bring peace to our world in whatever ways we are able. This has to be our prime motivation and intention.

如果我们想要以一种促进内心平静、精神和谐的方式来培养我们的自我意识,就必须学会真实面对自己。我们要有意识地努力成为一个有智慧、对他人有同情心的并匡扶正义的人,同时竭尽所能的保护身边的人、治愈周围的人,为世界带来和平。这才应该是我们做任何事的最终动机和目的。

To gain true happiness the mind has to transcend to a new and higher level of understanding in which we begin to discover our inner soul and combine all our many senses to perceive everything that surrounds us. Only by being conscious of what we truly feel and understanding the source of these feelings in order to make better choices on how we live, can we understand what our soul is and what our role and purpose should be.

为了获得真正的幸福,我们的心智必须要超越到一个新的更高的理解层次。在这个层次中,我们开始发现自己的内在灵魂,并结合我们所有的感官来认识我们周围的一切。我们要有意识地去了解自己真正的感受,并理解这些感受出现的原因,以便在生活中做出更好的选择;只有这样我们才能理解自己的灵魂,才能明白自己所扮演的角色和自己的使命。

You don't have a soul.
You ARE a soul.
You have a body.

你没有灵魂。
你就是灵魂,
只是以身体作为载体。

This will gradually emerge from a proper awareness of all those feelings associated with each element of happiness and unhappiness that is experienced, together with an acceptance of life as it truly and honestly is, and of oneself as a mortal, humble and fallible human being trying nevertheless to do the best he or she can.

等你对所有经历的快乐和痛苦,逐渐产生正确的认识,并接受生活最原本、最真实的样子,接受自己只是一个谦卑的、易犯错误的但仍然尽全力做到最好的普通人。这个时候就能看到这一点。

Happiness is when what you think, what you say, and what you do are in harmony.
Vedic injunction

幸福就是你的所思、所言、所行保持和谐一致。
吠陀训诫

Awareness

认识

Developing an acute awareness of both the external world and our own internal mind and thoughts is essential.

培养我们对外部世界和自己内心思想的敏锐认识至关重要。

The external world includes everything that we experience as an outsider looking in. This includes all of the environment in which we live and that we observe; the seas, the mountains and valleys, the streams, the flowers, art, music, sculpture, poetry, prose, architecture, science and so on.

外部世界是指我们作为一个局外人所感受到的一切事物。这包括我们目前生活的和观察到的所有事物,如大海、山谷、小溪、鲜花、艺术、音乐、雕塑、诗歌、散文、建筑、科学等。

It also includes all those things that we observe unhappily; suffering, poverty, sickness, cruelty, neglect and anguish of all kinds, for which we need to develop a real sense of compassion and justice, not just a passing and short-lived reflection to assuage feelings of guilt.

除此之外,也包括我们所经历的所有不愉快的事情,如苦难、贫穷、疾病、残忍、忽视和各种痛苦。对此我们需要培养一种真正的同情心和正义感,而不仅仅是为了减轻负罪感而进行短暂的反思。

Have compassion for all beings, rich and poor alike; each has their suffering.

无论是穷人还是富人,每个人都遭受着不同的痛苦,因此我们要怜悯众生。

Developing a heightened awareness of our external world and inner mind is not at all easy. But that doesn't mean we shouldn't make the effort to keep trying and learning. Because herein lies the secret of inner harmony and peace.

通向幸福的阶梯

提高对外部世界和内心世界的认识并非易事,但这并不意味着我们应该停止尝试和学习,因为这是获得内心和谐与平静的秘径。

We need to develop our ability to concentrate and reflect deeply in order to appreciate the moment in which we find ourselves, without concerns about the past or fears about the future; just focusing on the present moment.

我们要培养自己专注和反思的能力,这样才能更好地认识自己所处的当下,而不必担心过往、惧怕将来;只专注于当下。

Do not dwell in the past, do not dream of the future, concentrate the mind on the present moment.
Buddhist sutra

不恋过往,不念未来,着眼当下。
佛经

By learning to concentrate on the present moment we gradually develop a better appreciation of all that surrounds us, of our friends, our family, our communities, right down to all the small but nevertheless significant elements that animate, enrich and gladden our lives.

学会了专注于当下,我们逐渐学会更好地理解和欣赏周围的一切,朋友、家人、社区,以及所有微不足道却对我们生活至关重要,让我们的生活丰富多彩、充满乐趣的一切点滴。

As we learn to appreciate more profoundly, with all our senses, what is all around us and what our true inner thoughts are, so we also start to develop a greater depth of feeling and understanding of who we are and of our universe.

随着我们逐渐学会用所有的感官更深刻地理解和欣赏周围的一切,更清楚地了解自己内心的真实想法,我们就会开始对我们是谁和我们的宇宙产生更深远地理解。

Too often, we are too busy in our daily lives to become consciously aware of what is going on around us and we miss out on the many opportunities for learning, reflecting, understanding and happiness.

有太多时候,我们因为日常的忙碌而无法主动地意识到周围的变化。于是,错过了许多学习、反思、理解和感受快乐的机会。

Being increasingly aware of what is going on inside our own mind, our true self, requires courage and honesty.

勇气和诚实能让我们不断意识到内心的想法和真实的自我。

We need to be mindful that we have a number of selves.

我们也不要忘记,人是由多个自我组成的。

There is the 'present' self that experiences the world, that is curious about its environment and that learns and absorbs. This is the first-person experience that is present during the waking day and can learn to be in the moment. It is where memories are first built and it is these memories that serve to fill out our personality.

有一个"当下的"自我生活在目前的世界,它对周围的一切充满好奇,并且不断学习、吸收新知识。它在每一个清醒的日子里,以第一人称体验的方式让我们学习活在当下。这是我们的记忆最初建立的地方,也正是这些记忆,逐渐填补了我们的个性空缺。

Throughout life we lay down memories as we experience interesting events and it is vital for health and well-being that we continue to do so into old age to guard against only living in the past and no longer living for anything in the present.

在我们的一生中,有趣好玩的事情留下的记忆让我们印象深刻,这些记忆对我们的身心健康至关重要。当我们步入老年之时,也应该继续不断尝试新鲜有趣的事情,这样才能防止我们只沉溺于过去而不再活在当下。

Then there is the 'private' self that talks to the conscious mind, leads, judges, ruminates, worries and controls. This is the self that is a function of all the past experiences, joys and sufferings and guides our conscious mind. It seeks to protect us by raising doubts, fears and hopes but it can also prevent us from seeing reality as it truly is. The private self contains all our past traumas and all those little black events that we have put at the back of our minds and would rather not recall.

然后是"私人的"自我,它和有意识的头脑进行对话、引导、判断、反思、担忧和控制。这是一个集所有过去经历、欢笑和痛苦于一身的自我,它可以引导我们的思想。它试图通过提出怀疑、感受恐惧、燃起希望的方式来保护我们,但它也能阻止我们看到现实的真面目。私人的自我包含了我们过去所有的创伤和所有那些我们放在脑后不想回忆的黑色小事件。

There is the 'public' self that shares with the rest of the world only that which it thinks it should. This is the image we like to present externally in the (often mistaken) belief that it will somehow beneficially enhance our status, the way people think of us and thus how we may think of ourselves. Where this self is not in sync with our private self, we experience disquiet and disharmony. If the image lacks authenticity, so too will our own self-belief and our own inner harmony will suffer.

接下来便是"公众的"自我,它只与人分享那些它认为应该分享的东西。"公众的"自我就是我们喜欢对外展示的个人形象,因为我们(往往错误地)相信,它会以某种方式提高我们的地位和别人对我们的评价,从而改变我们对自己的认识。当这个自我与私人的自我步调不一致时,忧虑与不和谐就产生了。如果这个对外的个人形象缺乏真实性,我们的自信和内心和谐也会受到冲击。

The 'remembered' self, unlike the present self, is the memory or story we have chosen to create about past events and tends to be not only different from reality but also heavily biased.

"记忆中的"自我与当下的自我不同,它是我们对过去事件创造的记忆或故事,往往与现实不同,而且带有严重的偏见。

When we experience something, whether positive or negative, we have certain sensations and emotions right there and then.

当我们经历了无论是积极还是消极的事情时,都会产生一定的感觉和情绪。

With the passage of time, however, we remember the occasion with different eyes and feelings. We 'remember' different aspects and begin to alter the picture to suit our needs with a heavy bias.

然而,随着时间的推移,我们以不同的眼光和感觉记住了那个时刻。我们"记住了"不同的方面,并开始带着严重的偏见来改变我们记忆中的画面,以此来适应自己的需要。

If we experienced a wonderful holiday but the return journey included delays, returning to a different airport, and so on, we may well recall the holiday as 'a bit of a disaster' giving much heavier bias to the few hours of pain compared to the many days of enjoyment.

假设我们刚刚结束了一个美好的假期,但在回程途中却经历了航班延误、更改机场等突发情况。下一次回想起这个假期时,我们心中总会觉得这次假期"有那么一点不愉快",与享受了许多天的快乐相比,这几小时的痛苦给我们的记忆带来了巨大的偏差。

Similarly, if we experienced a negative event—for example, we stumbled and fell at the end of a mountain climb but with no real harm done (other than to pride)—our remembered self creates a story of heroism in the face of adversity, which will animate many a future conversation.

同样,当我们经历了一件负面消极的事情时:比如,爬山的过程中不小心跌倒了,但没有对身体造成什么实质性的伤害(除了自尊心有些受伤)。于是,记忆中的自我创造了一个面对逆境的英雄故事,平添了几分谈资。

If we drive over-aggressively on the motorway and exchange 'niceties' with another driver, we know at the time that we are in the wrong but subsequent recollections and what we may say to others about the incident will tend to cast the blame on the other driver.

如果我们在高速公路上超速开车,还和另一个司机交流超速"心得"。虽然当时自己就明白这种行为是错误的,但在随后的回忆或与他人的谈话中,我们很可能会把责任推卸给另一个司机。

The remembered self can also confuse itself into thinking that we participated in events that happened to others but only happened to us in our mind. It is said that, as time passes, we have more and more vivid recollections of events that never happened.

记忆中的自我时常也会把我们自己绕晕,让我们误以为自己参与了发生在别人身上的事,但实际上这件事只在我们的脑海中出现过。据说,随着时间的流逝,我们会对从未发生过的事情产生越来越生动的回忆。

These examples are simple and relatively trivial.

这些事例很简单,甚至都是些微不足道的小事。

But the remembered self, if uncontrolled or too self-serving, can be much more nefarious, leading to serious issues of self-deception, pride, anger, blame and sadness and these can easily destroy relationships and the inner peace we are so diligently seeking to attain.

但记忆中的自我如果失去了控制或过于自私,就会变得极其邪恶,导致自我欺骗、骄纵、易怒、推卸责任和悲伤过度等严重问题。这些问题很容易将我们努力寻求的关系和内心平静付之一炬。

If we are to accede to the happiness of harmony, we need to be clear and truthful about our 'selves' and take very careful note of what is happening in our minds with absolute honesty. Only with honesty and truth can we grow to become better people.

想要获得和谐的幸福,我们需要对我们的"自我"保持清醒和真诚,并以绝对诚实的态度仔细记录我们头脑中发生的事情。只有诚实和真理,能让我们称为更好的人。

The alternative is to keep deceiving ourselves and simply living lies. This makes learning and progress impossible and destroys happiness.

另外一个选择就是继续自我欺骗,继续就这么地生活在谎言中。这么一来学习和进步就无从谈起了,幸福感也被破坏无疑。

You cannot improve what you have persuaded yourself to believe is perfectly alright or cannot see in the first place.

一件事情,如果你认定已经完美,或者根本没有看到有问题,就不可能做出任何改善。

When we criticize others, feel envious, resentful, angry, overlooked, unloved, alone, we are only hurting ourselves and allowing the emotions from our own imaginings of the motives of others to unbalance our inner harmony.

如果批判他人时,我们只是感到嫉妒、怨恨、愤怒、被忽视、不被爱、孤独的话,我们只是在伤害自己,任由自己对他人动机的想象所产生的情绪来破坏我们内心的和谐。

We are allowing these unchecked emotions to rule our heart and damage our soul through lack of discipline.

我们任由这些不加约束的情绪控制自己的内心,并因缺乏自律而损害我们的灵魂。

> ***A disciplined mind brings happiness.***
> **Buddha**

> **自律带来幸福。**
> **佛陀**

We need, in a disciplined way, to take time to become aware of and identify each emotion that overtakes us. We need then to examine carefully where the emotion has come from, why we feel the way we do, whether it is appropriate or justified and, if not, what learning we can gain and what we should do to manage better the effects of these emotions in the future.

我们,应当以一种谨慎的方式,花时间去认识和识别每一种控制我们的情绪。然后,仔细审查这每一种情绪从何而来,为什么我们会产生这种感觉,它的产生是否合乎情理。如果答案是否定的,我们可以从中学到什么?我们应该怎么做,才能更好地管理这些情绪在未来可能带来的影响。

If we decide that the emotion is not justified, did we allow it to be created by our subconscious mind and then grow out of all proportion? If it was unhelpful to us, what was it that triggered it? In what way was it disruptive to us? When we attributed our anger or frustration to the actions of others, were we right to do so or were we simply reflecting our own inadequacies and needs? What can we learn and what can we do differently to promote our inner harmony rather than subconsciously destroy it?

如果这种情绪的出现是不合情理的。那么,是我们自己任由它被潜意识所创造并延续的吗?如果这种情绪对我们毫无帮助,那又是什么触发了它?它对我们有什么样的破坏性?当我们把自己的愤怒或挫折归咎于他人的行为时,这样做合适吗?还是说这种做法仅仅反映了我们自己的缺陷和需求?我们能从中学到什么?我们能做出哪些改变来促进内心的和谐,而不是下意识地去破坏?

Whenever you are about to find fault with someone, ask yourself the following question: what fault of mine most nearly resembles the one I am about to criticize?
Marcus Aurelius

每次你要挑别人的错处时,先扪心自问自己有没有和他犯相似的错误。
马可·奥勒留

Acceptance

接受

Once we become more aware of our emotions and what their causes and effects are, we come to realize again the Buddhist and Stoic principle that the only aspects of our life that we can really control are our thoughts and our actions and that there is little point in worrying about, let alone attempt to impact, what we cannot control.

一旦我们对自己的情绪及其成因、后果有了更多的了解,我们会再次回到到佛教和斯多葛学派的原则,即"我们在生活中真正能掌控的只有自己的思想和行为"。因此,担心我们无法控制的事情毫无意义,更不用说试图影响我们无法控制的事情了。

Paradoxically, although we will still care deeply about many things, unless we develop, at the same time, a sense of indifference about what we cannot influence or control, we will not be able to focus on what we can affect positively, and we will thus be unable to achieve inner peace or harmony.

这是一个矛盾体,一方面我们对很多事情非常在乎;另一方面,仍然需要对那些在自己影响或掌控之外的事情选择放手。不然的话，我们就无法把精力放在能够产生积极影响的事情上，也因此不能达到内心的和谐与平静。

We have to learn to accept this and to realize that attempting to control what is outside our sphere of influence is a waste of energy and effort and ultimately self-defeating. It is damaging to ourselves and to our external world.

我们要学会接受这一点，认识到试图去掌控我们影响力之外的事物是徒劳的，最终反而会事与愿违。损耗我们自己的内心和外部的世界。

> *We cannot control the impressions others form about us, and the effort to do so only debases our character.*
> **Sharon Lebell**

> 我们无法控制别人对我们的印象，
> 试图去控制只会降低我们的品格。
> 沙伦·莱贝尔

> *Remove the judgment, and you have removed the thought 'I am hurt': remove the thought 'I am hurt', and the hurt itself is removed.*
> **Marcus Aurelius**

摈弃你的评判,你就丢开了"我受到了伤害"这种抱怨:
摈弃"我受到了伤害"这种抱怨,这伤害也就消失了。
马可·奥勒留

***There is only one way to happiness
and that is to cease worrying about things
which are beyond the power of our will.*
Epictetus**

只有一个方法可以获得幸福,
那就是停止担忧那些我们无法控制的事情。
埃皮克提图

Acceptance is close to letting go in that it requires us to stop fretting about what others are thinking, being anxious about our image or stressed about what others are or are not saying about us.

接受就像放手一样,它要求我们停止为别人的想法而烦恼,不再为自己的形象而焦虑,不再为别人对我们的评论或闭口不言而感到压力。

As long as we are true to ourselves and living a life whose intention is compassion, peace and love, we can be confident that we are doing the best we can for our own inner peace, the harmony of our soul and our universe.

只要我们忠于自己,以一种充满同情、平静、和谐为目的的心情生活,就能够确信我们正在为达到内心平静、灵魂同宇宙的和谐而竭尽全力。

Allowing external factors outside our control to determine our feelings and our life is a recipe for disharmony and unhappiness. If we feel resentful or angry at another or envious of their achievement, we are allowing them to control our emotions. And they probably don't care anyway! This is the path of fear and doubt, rather than love and peace.

让我们无法控制的外部因素来决定自己的感情和生活,是不和谐与不快乐产生的根源。如果我们对某人产生了怨恨或愤怒,或嫉妒他人取得的成就,我们就被这些情绪所掌控了。而那些让你产生怨恨、愤怒或嫉妒情绪的人可能根本就不在乎你的想法!那么,这就成了一条通往恐惧和怀疑的道路,而不是爱与和平之路。

We cannot harbour such emotions and at the same time experience inner harmony.

我们不可能在心怀这种情绪的同时,还体验到内心和谐的快乐。

If you ever happen to turn your attention to externals, so as to wish to please anyone, be assured

*that you have ruined your scheme of life.
Be contented, then, in everything with
being a philosopher; and, if you wish to be
thought so likewise by anyone, appear so to
yourself, and it will suffice you.*
Epictetus

如果你曾经把自己的注意力放到身外,并希望以此取悦于他人,你就已经毁了自己的生活。像哲学家一样满足吧。以哲学的态度去处事;如果你希望别人也这么看待你,就先表现出来,你自然就会满足。
埃皮克提图

Acceptance means understanding and accepting ourselves for who we are, with all our faults and failings. Facing up to who we are with honesty, modesty and clear-sightedness is the first step to enable us to learn to be better people by working on those areas that are causing imbalances and disharmony.

接受意味着理解和接受我们真正的自己,包括所有犯过的错误和失败。以诚实、谦虚、清晰的眼光看待自己,这是我们通过研究那些导致我们内心不平衡、不和谐的领域,来学习成为更好的人的第一步。

*Waste no more time arguing
about what a good man should be. Be one.*
Marcus Aurelius

通向幸福的阶梯

**不要再浪费时间去争论好人应该怎么做。
自己做一个好人吧。
马可·奥勒留**

Learning to live in harmony with oneself means taking the trouble to think about how to be a better person, setting personal goals and practising being that person.

学会与自己和谐相处意味着要不厌其烦地思考如何成为一个更好的人,为自己确定个人目标并为目标的实现而努力。

Becoming a good person through understanding, compassion and justice is what the Greek philosophers, Socrates, Plato and Aristotle promulgated and this is also the philosophy of the Stoics. It is also the foundation precept of most religions.

通过开发自己的理解力、同情心和正义感成为一个好人是古希腊的哲学家、苏格拉底、柏拉图和亚里士多德和斯多葛学派所倡导的思想,也是大多数宗教的基本教义。

It is only by becoming a better person that we can live in harmony and peace with ourselves. It is only by living in harmony and peace with ourselves that we can live in harmony with the universe and experience the true happiness of harmony.

只有成为一个更好的人，我们才能与自己和谐相处。只有与自己和谐相处，才能与宇宙和谐相处，体验到真正的和谐的幸福。

He who lives in harmony with himself lives in harmony with the universe.

与自己相处和谐的人才能同宇宙和谐相处。

Savouring the moment

活在当下

Being in the moment, being aware, accepting who we are and the people we are with, without judgment and with reverence and humility, allows us to savour each precious moment with family and friends in a way that transcends the everyday and reaches higher levels of joy.

活在当下，正确地认识自己，接受真实的自己和我们身边的人。以尊敬谦卑之心，并不带任何评判的心态，以一种超越日常生活和达到更高快乐层次的方式，享受与家人和朋友在一起的美妙时刻。

Consider these scenes:

想象一下这样的场景：

A family is together, after dinner, sitting on a sofa facing the fire. The grandparents are cuddling the grandchildren who are about to read a children's book before going to bed. The parents are looking on with happiness in their hearts. The children take it in turns to read a page of the book. Occasionally they stumble on a word and are helped through it. Their imagination is stimulated by what they are reading and they are, themselves, fully in the moment too and savouring each second. They continually touch the hand of their grandparents for the warmth of human contact. They occasionally glance at the fire with its dancing flames. They look up at their parents and exchange loving smiles. As they become happily sleepy, a grandparent takes over reading the last page or two. They go to bed and are asleep almost immediately. All have experienced a moment of magic, of pure unadulterated joy and of harmony.

晚饭过后,一家人围着炉火坐在沙发上。祖父母搂着正在看儿童读本的孙子孙女,父母坐在一旁满心欢喜地看着他们。孩子们轮流朗读,偶尔碰到不认识的词,再求助大人。书本中的内容激发了孩子的想象力,而孩子们也被书本的内容完全所吸引,沉浸于其中。孩子们不断地抚摸着祖父母的手,体会与人接触的温暖。偶尔,他们瞥一眼在火炉里跳动的火焰,或者抬起头和父母默契地对视。等到孩子们读着读着睡着了,大人接过书,读完最后的两页。合上书,大家都去睡觉,一躺下就进入了梦乡。这一切如此美妙,就像童话故事里,一个充满喜悦与和谐的时刻。

Two colleagues are having a meeting with several others. The subject matter is difficult and significant but fascinating, and both are as curious to learn and understand as they are to contribute to the decision. While they are clearly on a similar wavelength and know it, they recognize and celebrate the fact that, not having the same experiences, they have different skills to bring to the party. They respect each other's point of view completely and support each other unconditionally when they share the same perspective. There are no hidden motives between them. They are not in the business of scoring points or appearing to be cleverer than they are. When they feel they need to change their mind about something because they accept a better argument, they do so openly and without shame or embarrassment. They are looking for the best outcome. They have complete trust. They hardly need to exchange words as a look says it all. They are living a moment of friendship and harmony.

有两个同事正在和其他几人一起开会,这次会议的主题既困难又重要,同时极具吸引力。作为决策者中的一员,他们两都抱着好奇心去学习和理解。显然,他们感觉到对方和自己气场相投,但又认识到,也庆幸各自有着不同的经历和技能,可以运用到这个议题上。在观点一致的时候,他们完全尊重对方,并无条件地支持他。在他们之间,没有隐瞒或遮掩的,也不是为了在商业上争个高低,也不是为了表现自己比对方聪明。一旦感觉自己因为接受了一个比原有思路更好的观点,需要改变思路时,他们会公开地接受他人的观点,并不会感到丝毫的羞耻或尴尬。他们在寻求最好的结果,对彼此有完完全全的信任。他们之间几乎不需要互相交换意见,一个眼神就能说明一切。此刻的他们,就在享受友谊的默契与和谐。

Being able to savour each moment to the full is one of the greatest joys that human beings can experience, wherever, whenever and with whomsoever that may be. It arises from an awareness of the significance of any moment experienced in a spirit of inner calm and peace.

不论何时何地与谁在一起,能够把当下享受到极致是人类能够体验的喜悦的最大限度。它的起点是对任何一个时刻的重要性的认知。

Controlling ego and self-talk

自我控制和"自我对话"

Savouring each precious moment, learning to accept, enjoy and be enthusiastic about such moments in our life and attaining the happiness of harmony requires an understanding of our ego and its pervasive and damaging nature.

品味每一个珍贵的时刻,学会接受、享受这些时刻,并对生活中的这些时刻报以热情,最终获得和谐的幸福,就需要我们对"自我"和它的广泛性和破坏性具备一定的了解。

It is simply not possible to attain this harmony if our ego-driven self-talk is allowed to govern our thinking in the way it does, without proper control. Our self-talk, we will recall, is that little voice that is constantly chatting to us based on all our previous experiences and seeking to 'protect' us by keeping us 'the way we are.'

如果我们放任,由着"自我"驱动的"自我对话"主导我们的思维,不加以适当的控制,那么基本就不可能达到这种和谐。回想一下,"自我对话"就是那种小小的声音,它不断地根据我们过往的经历与我们聊天,并试图通过保持我们的"本来面目"来"保护"我们。

But keeping us the way we are is not always good. In the case of people who have become alcoholics, for example, keeping them the way they are is not helpful. Left unchecked, the self-talk of an alcoholic will say, 'It's ok to have a drink.' 'Only one drink can't do any harm.' 'We'll stop tomorrow.' Without changing our self-talk through re-programming the mind and often, such as in the case of alcoholics and similar addictions, medical treatment, our self-talk will create disharmony and make it impossible to find peace, calm and happiness.

但是保持我们的现状并不总是件好事。例如,对于那些酗酒的人来说,让他们保持现状是没有任何好处的。如果不加以控制,酗酒者的"自我对话"内容就是"喝一杯没关系"、"就喝一杯差不到哪儿去"、"明天就戒"。如果不通过重新规划思维来改变我们的"自我对话", 就如酗酒者和类似的成瘾者,沉迷医学治疗的人,""自我"对话"就会造成不和谐,使人无法得到安宁、平静和幸福。

When we think deeply about it, however, most of our self-talk's interventions are ego-driven. Our self-talk is accustomed to encouraging us to say and do things that gain us advantage in some way or another and thus feed our ego. We want, crave even, to be successful, admired, loved and cherished, and to be winners, etc., and our self-talk feeds this need.

深入思考一下你会发现,"自我对话"的大部分干预都是由"自我"驱动的。我们的"自我对话"习惯鼓励我们去说,去做一些为自己带来好处的事情,从而来满足我们的"自我"。我们"想要",甚至"渴望"成功,"渴望"被人敬仰、被爱、被珍视、成为赢家等等,而我们的"自我对话"满足了这种需要。

Our self-talk helps us to act and say what it thinks will benefit us, based on past experience, and, unless it is overridden by our conscious mind, most of it will be self-serving. For example, if we want to impress so that others think well of us in order to feed our ego, we will speak half-truths, make up stories, even blatantly lie, and act dishonestly or in a way designed to deceive in order to create the 'right' impression. If, for example, we want to make a sale and boost our image as master salespeople, to inflate our pride and ego by giving the impression that we are better than others, we will be tempted to tell only part of the sales story and not paint a totally honest picture. How often do we read about events where people have been deliberately misled at great personal cost?

"自我对话",会根据以往的经验,帮助我们做出对自己有利的事情,说出对自己有利的话,除非它被我们的意识所覆盖,否则大部分的"自我对话"都是为"自我"服务的。例如,我们想要给别人留下一个好印象,这样对方会对我们产生好印象,最终满足我们的"自我",我们就会说半真半假的话,编造故事,甚至明目张胆的撒谎,以不诚实地方式行事,或者为了制造"正确"的印象而故意欺骗。例如,我们想要达成一笔交易,提升自己作为销售大师的形象,给人留下一种我们比他人更好的印象,以此来夸大我们的自尊心和"自我",那么我们就会倾向于只讲述销售故事的一部分,而不是描述出完全真实的画面。生活中不乏这样故意误导别人,而因此付出了巨大的个人代价的例子。

None of this helps our self-esteem, our self-image or our self-love. And if we cannot love ourselves because of such attitudes, how can we love others? If our ego is constantly encouraging us to win and have our way, we cannot live an honest life or in a state of peace. Only by becoming 'gentle' or ego-less can we achieve a sense of calm and harmony.

这些对增强我们的自尊心,提升"自我"形象或促进我们的自爱都没有多少帮助。如果我们因为这样的态度而做不到爱自己,又如何去爱别人呢?如果我们的"自我"不断地鼓励我们要赢,要按照自己的方式行事,我们就不能过上诚实的生活或保持一个和谐的状态。只有变得"温和"或放下"自我",我们才能获得平静与和谐的感觉。

Blessed are the gentle,
for they shall inherit the earth.
Matthew 5:5, World English Bible

温柔的人有福了,他们必承受地土。
马太福音第5章5节,《世界英语圣经》

We need to be very conscious and mindful of what we say and do and constantly, critically and with discipline examine our thoughts and deeds ('the unexamined life is not worth living') to ensure that we are acting and speaking honourably, wisely, compassionately and with love.

我们需要非常有意识地去注意自己的言行,并不断地、批判性地、有纪律地审视自己的思想和行为("没有经过审视的人生是不值得的"),以确保我们的言行都得体、明智、有同情心的、充满爱。

***Man, know thyself,
and you are going to know the gods.***

人啊,了解你自己,你就会了解神。

As we learn to understand and control our ego, live more 'in the moment' and just focus on that, without allowing thoughts of past concerns or future fears to stress our minds or feed our egos, we let go of our tensions, start to enjoy life and begin to really feel and experience the happiness of harmony.

学会理解并控制"自我",更多地"活在当下"、专注于此,不让过去的担忧或未来的恐惧给我们的精神带来压力或满足我们的"自我",我们就会放下紧张,开始享受生活,开始真正感受和体验和谐的幸福。

You will enjoy any activity in which you are fully present, any activity that is not just a means to an end. It isn't the action you perform that you really enjoy, but the deep sense of aliveness that flows into it ... This means that when you enjoy doing something, you are really experiencing the

joy of Being in its dynamic aspect. That's why anything you enjoy doing connects you with the power behind all creation … If you feel your life lacks significance or is too stressful or tedious, it is because you haven't brought that dimension into your life yet. Being conscious in what you do has not yet become your main aim.
Eckhart Tolle

不论做什么,只要你全身心投入,都能享受其中,任何不只是为了达到目的的活动。你真正享受的并不是你所做的事情,而是其中蕴含的强烈的活力……也就是说你真正享受做某件事情时,你实际上是享受置身其中的那种喜悦。也正因此,你喜欢做的任何事情都能让你感受到创造背后的力量……如果你觉得自己的生活缺乏意义,压力太大或太单调,那是因为你还没有把那个维度带入自己的生活。有意识地体验自己所做的事情还没有成为你的主要目标。
埃克哈特·托利

Purpose and intention

目的和初衷

What, then, is our purpose in life? How important are our intentions?

那么,我们的人生目的是什么?我们的初衷有多重要?

Intentions are like goals and they will drive our purpose in life. Until we have intentions we simply drift. As we develop our goals and intentions, we exercise choice—'I intend to do this'—and we always have a choice.

初衷就像是目标,驱动着我们向人生的目的地前行。在我们拥有初衷之前,我们只是在随波逐流。有了目标和初衷,我们就开始进行选择——"我打算要这样做"——我们总是有选择的。

We can decide to choose a path of fear and doubt, where we see the world as a place where only the fittest survive. Or we can choose a path of love and compassion, where we see the world as a place where we can help, support and protect our fellow human beings, our world and the universe—now and for future generations.

我们可以选择一条充满恐惧和疑虑的道路,在这条道路上,我们看到的世界就是一个只有适者才可以生存的地方。又或者我们可以选择一条充满爱和同情新的道路,这条路上我们可以帮助、支持和保护我们的人类同胞、我们的世界和宇宙——以及现在和未来的世世代代。

Our intentions create our reality. If our intentions are founded on the belief that the world is essentially inimical and to be feared, we will reflect this in the choices we make and expressions of anger, guilt, shame, resentment and unhappiness.

我们的初衷造就了我们的现实世界。如果我们的初衷建立在这样一种信念上,即这个世界本质上是充满敌意的、令人畏惧的,那么我们在做出选择和表达愤怒、内疚、羞耻、怨恨和不快时,就会反映出这一点。

If, on the other hand, our intentions are founded on the belief that the world is essentially good, loving and forgiving, we will make decisions and exercise choices that are designed to create harmony and love.

相反,如果我们的初衷是建立在相信世界本质上是美好的、充满爱和宽容的基础上,我们做出的决定和选择就会以创造和谐与爱为目的。

If we believe that we are not responsible for the consequences of our intentions and we behave as though we can remain unaffected by what we do, then the actions we take will reflect this and our world will suffer.

如果我们认为自己不必为自己的行为所导致的后果负任何责任,并且表现得好像对自己毫无影响,那么我们做的事情将会反映出这一点,我们所在的世界也会因此遭殃。

If we believe it is alright to misuse our scientific discoveries for destructive purposes, we should not be surprised if the damage we create reaches horrific dimensions.

如果我们认为滥用科学发现来达到破坏性的目的是正常的,那么就我们的破坏造成的损害程度也就不足为奇了。

If, on the other hand, we believe that scientific discoveries should be used to protect our environment, to heal, to house, to feed, to educate, to nurture, to sustain our world, we are choosing a path of compassion and love.

另一方面,如果我们认为科学应该用来保护环境、治愈他人、解决住房问题、解决粮食问题、解决教育问题、培育人才、实现可持续发展,那我们选择的是一条充满同情和爱的道路。

If we believe it is right to take, and take, and take again everything we can without concern for its effect on other people or the environment, make as much money we can irrespective of the fact this may impoverish many less fortunate than ourselves, cheat and steal at will and take everything we can from the earth while discarding our rubbish indiscriminately and without thought for future generations, we are choosing a path of fear and doubt.

如果我们认为我们可以不断地、尽可能地索取一切,而不考虑对他人或环境造成的影响,我们可以不放过任何一个赚钱的机会,而不顾这样做可能会导致不如我们幸运的人变得贫穷,我们可以随意地欺骗和偷窃,不停地从地球上夺走一切,随意地丢弃垃圾,不为我们的子孙后代考虑,那么我们就是选择了一条充满恐惧和疑虑的道路。

If, on the other hand, we believe that we have an absolute responsibility for protecting our species, our families, our friends and our universe, nurturing and teaching our children and helping to create a world of peace and harmony, we are choosing a path of peace, unity and happiness.

相反,如果我们认为自己有绝对的责任来保护我们的物种、我们的家庭、我们的朋友和我们的宇宙,抚养和教育我们的儿童,创建一个充满平静与和谐的世界,我们就是在选择一条平和、团结和幸福的道路。

Is it not our duty to enter into a sacred and spiritual pledge with ourselves and with like-minded souls to encourage as many as possible to follow a path of love and compassion, rather than one of fear and doubt? Would this not result in a better world? Or is it all too late? Have we so damaged ourselves and our world that a return to truth, honesty and inner peace is no longer possible?

我们难道没有责任是与自己志同道合的灵魂达成一个神圣的精神承诺,以鼓励尽可能多的人走上爱和同情的道路,而不是充满恐惧和疑虑的道路。这难道不会带来一个更美好的世界吗?还是已经为时已晚?我们是否已经太过于破坏了我们生活的世界,以至于不再可能回归到充满真理、诚实和内心平静的环境?

The Greek philosophers believed that it was always possible, by living a life of wisdom and virtue, to create a better, less selfish, more tolerant, more just and happier society and world. There are still very many good people who are fighting for these values and for justice.

希腊哲学家相信,践行智慧和美德的生活,可以创造出一个拥有更多美好、更少自私、更多宽容、更加公正、更为幸福的社会和世界。现在仍然有很多这样怀有美好愿望的人为这些价值观和正义奋斗着。

Is it not our role also to promote constructive positive change and to become agents for good ourselves? With effort we can all make a difference to our lives and to the lives of others and bring peace, harmony and concord to our world.

我们的作用不也是促进建设性的积极变化,并成为促进自身发展的推动者吗? 通过努力,我们都可以改变自己的生活,改变他人的生活,给我们的世界带来平静、和谐与和睦。

Should this not be our true purpose?

难道这不是我们真正的目的所在吗?

Wisdom, reverence, compassion and love

智慧、尊重、同情、爱

The happiness of harmony is the achievement of sufficient wisdom, reverence, compassion and love to be committed to the growth, peace and happiness of others and of our world.

和谐带来的幸福是足够的智慧、尊重、同情和爱,注入到他人和这个世界的成长、平静与幸福中带来的成就。

It starts with ourselves. If we feel compassion for ourselves, we will feel compassion for others. If we have respect and love for ourselves, we will feel and project respect and love for others. If we can forgive ourselves, we will forgive others. If we learn wisdom, we will be able to impart wisdom to others.

它始于我们自身。如果我们对自己有同情心,就会对他人产生同情心;如果我们尊重爱护自己,就会尊重爱护他人;如果我们能够原谅自己,就能够原谅他人;如果我们学习了智慧,就能向他人传授智慧。

The happiness of harmony is the happiness that comes from being at one and at peace with ourselves and our universe. From there we can help, support and nurture others so that they may find their own inner peace; and empower them to make their contribution in turn.

和谐的幸福是自己和宇宙合二为一、和谐相处的幸福。从这一点出发，我们可以帮助他人、支持他人、培养他人，这样，他们就能找到自己内心的平静，具备为别的人做出贡献的能力。

The answer to the questions 'Who am I?' and 'Why am I here?' should now be much clearer: 'Who am I?' I am a person whose soul, 'a particle of love', is a small fragment of the universe and the 'eternal source' to which I will return … like everyone else. 'Why am I here?' I am here because I wish to be a good person who leaves the world in a better state than it was when I entered it; to have created happiness and joy for those with whom I have had the privilege of sharing my life; to have helped, supported, nurtured, comforted, enjoyed and loved unconditionally, with respect and humility; to have moved closer to the light of universal knowledge that comes from continual reflection, the wisdom and the energy to listen and change, and a state of inner peace and harmony.

至此,"我是谁?","我为什么在这里?"的答案应该更加清晰了:"我是谁?",我是一个人,我的灵魂,也就是"爱的分子",是这个宇宙中的一个小碎片,是我和其他人一样终究要回归的"永恒之源"的一部分…"我为什么在这里?",我来这里是因为我想要做一个好人,一个可以让世界比我来之前变得更美好的好人;为了给那些我有幸与之共度一生的人创造幸福和快乐,以尊重和谦卑的态度给予他们无条件地帮助、支持、培养、安慰、享受和热爱,通过不断地反思,向普世知识之光靠拢,向倾听与改变的智慧和能量,向内在的平静与和谐靠拢。

To love another person is to see the face of God.

爱一个人就是通过他/她看到上帝

You find peace, not by rearranging the circumstances of your life, but by realizing who you are at the deepest level.
Eckhart Tolle

安宁不是来自对外界生活的重置,而是找到
最深层次的自己。
埃特哈克·托利

Are you aware of your impact on others? On yourself? Are you forgiving? To others? To yourself? Have you learned from your pain? Are you compassionate and kind? Do you realize the power

of our wake? Can you learn from unanticipated uncertainties in your life? Can you grow from struggle? Can you embrace your ego?
Can you embrace your own unconditional love? Do you leave ojas (sweet nectar) instead of ama (toxic residue) when you exit a room, a job, a relationship, this life? And what do you do once you realize you have left ama?
Davidji

你是否意识到自己对他人的影响？或者对自己的影响？你能原谅他人吗？或者能原谅自己？你从痛苦学到什么吗？你有同情心吗？你善良吗？你意识到我们觉醒的力量吗？你能从生活中无法预料的不确定性中学习吗？你能从挣扎中成长吗？你能拥抱""自我""吗？你能拥抱自己无条件的爱吗？当你离开一个房间、一份工作，从一段关系中走出，甚至从人的这一生离开时，你能留下甜蜜的回忆（ojas）而不是痛苦的过往（ama）吗？一旦意识到自己留下的都是痛苦的过去，你会怎么做呢？
戴维吉

The Stairway to Happiness is a message of hope and love.

《通向幸福的阶梯》传达的是希望和爱的讯息。

In a world which seems increasingly stressful, dangerous and unjust, it is easy to feel despondent and a deep sense of despair. After all, how can we seek happiness for ourselves when there is so much suffering in the world? It is almost as if we have no right to be happy when so many are unhappy!

在一个压力越来越大,充满危险和不公的世界,人们很容易感到沮丧和深深的绝望。无可否认,如果人世间有这么多的苦难,我们该如何为自己寻找幸福?那么多人都不开心,我们似乎也没有让自己快乐的权利!

The whole point of The Stairway to Happiness is to explain what happiness is, how it is created and achieved and how it can be used for good purposes and, above all, to help others.

《通向幸福的阶梯》这本书的目的就是为了阐释幸福的含义:幸福如何产生,如何实现的,如何知之而善用,最重要的是,能帮助他人实现幸福。

We can only start to be truly happy ourselves when we learn to understand that it is through helping others and awakening to what is real and authentic, rather than false and destructive, that we can begin the repairing process.

只有当我们明白,通过帮助他人,觉醒并懂得区分真实与虚假,本真与破坏性,我们才能开始"自我"修复的过程,才能感受到真正的幸福。

Creating Happiness is about action, not inaction; about being positive, not negative; about doing rather than complaining; about love and light rather than anger and hatred; about acting with tolerance, respect, cooperation and kindness, rather than selfishness, lack of concern, cynicism and isolation. It is about setting a personal example.

创造幸福需要我们行动起来，而不是被动等待；要积极向上，而不是消极悲观；需要付出实际行动，而不是一味地怨天尤人；要去爱，去点亮，而不是愤怒和怨恨；要带着宽容和尊重、合作和友善去行动，而不是怀揣自私自利、欠缺考虑、愤世嫉俗、孤立他人。幸福的创造需要树立起个人榜样。

There is a lot of beauty to life and it is the privilege, not to say the duty, of those who can see it to help others see it too, by helping, teaching and healing in whatever way possible.

生活中有许许多多美好的东西，那些能够看到这些美好的人，且不说责任，他们具备帮助他人发现这种美好的优势。通过帮助他人、教导他人、治愈他人，让他们也能发现生活中的美好。

If awakening to the reality of the cruelty and injustice in our world creates inner turmoil in our soul, then bringing happiness through active service and love for others is the surest way for us to bring peace and harmony.

如果说认识到这个世界的残酷和不公会在我们的灵魂深处激起不安,那么通过积极地对他人的关爱带来快乐,就是我们获得宁静与和谐的最可靠的方法。

We may well not be able to save the world. That doesn't mean we shouldn't try. Even if we, individually and collectively, only help one person achieve happiness, it will have been of value to that person and to the universe. That is the core message and aspiration of the book.

我们也许做不到拯救世界,但并不意味着我们应该放弃尝试。即使我们个人也好,集体也好,只帮助到了一个人获得幸福,那么,对这个人来说,对这个宇宙都是有价值的。这就是整本书想要传达的主旨和心声。

Helping one person won't change the whole world. But it could change the whole world for that one person. Think what would happen if we all started helping one person every day, every month, every year!

帮助一个人并不能改变整个世界,但却可能改变这个人的整个世界。试想一下,如果我们每个人每天、每个月、每一年都开始帮助一个人,那将会带来多大的改变!

Smiling is the language of angels Laughter is the music of happiness Kindness is the touch of the divine Love is the essence of the Soul

微笑是天使的语言,笑声是幸福的音乐,善良是神圣的触摸,爱是灵魂的本质

ABOUT THE AUTHOR
\关于作者

Vernon Sankey was born in France and educated in the UK. He graduated in Modern Languages at Oriel College, Oxford. He went straight from university into industry and spent the next 28 years in various countries, culminating as chief executive of a major international corporation in the UK.

作者卫尚凯(Vernon Sanky)出生于法国,在英国念书长大。毕业于牛津奥瑞尔学院的现代语言专业。毕业后便进入了商界,此后的28年里走遍了不同国度,后担任英国一家大型跨国公司的首席执行官。

He then became a non-executive director and chairman of several large and small international companies, and is still active in this field today. During this time he has also lectured on leadership and motivation at universities, schools and conferences.

卫尚凯先后任职于多家规模不等的跨国公司,担任非执行董事和董事长,至今仍活跃于商界。在此期间,他还在高校、学校和各大型会议上讲授领导力和动力。

In 1999 he co-founded a coaching and mentoring company where he further developed his knowledge of cognitive psychology to help mentor business executives as well as people in all walks of life.

1999年,他与合伙人共同创办了培训公司,进一步拓展自己在认知心理学方面的研究,并应用到企业高管指导和培训上,帮助自各行各业的人士。

The Stairway to Happiness is the product of this learning. Vernon is married with four children and five grandchildren. He lives in Berkshire.

《通向幸福的阶梯》正是作者学习成长后作品。卫尚凯已婚,育有四个子女。他也是五个孩子的祖父。卫尚凯目前定居伯克郡。

www.ingramcontent.com/pod-product-compliance
Lightning Source LLC
Chambersburg PA
CBHW071950070526
44583CB00015B/1130